THE 11:45 CALL

AN EXPOSITORY BIBLE STUDY OF THE BOOK OF JUDE

JOEL F. BLAKELY AND BRENDA KLUTZ BLAKELY

WESTBOW
PRESS
A DIVISION OF THOMAS NELSON

Scripture quotations taken from the New American Standard Bible®, Copyright © 1960, 1962, 1963, 1968, 1971, 1972, 1973, 1975, 1977, 1995 by The Lockman Foundation. Used by permission." (www.Lockman.org)

All scripture is from the NKJV unless otherwise noted.

The cover design is by Brenda Klutz Blakely. It was executed by Westbow Press staff.

The cover background image is an original photograph, titled Daybreak, from the photo-art collection by Joel F. Blakely, an internationally recognized photo artist.

WestBow Press books may be ordered through booksellers or by contacting:

WestBow Press
A Division of Thomas Nelson
1663 Liberty Drive
Bloomington, IN 47403
www.westbowpress.com
1-(866) 928-1240

ISBN: 978-1-4497-5049-7 (hc)
ISBN: 978-1-4497-5048-0 (sc)
ISBN: 978-1-4497-5047-3 (e)

Library of Congress Control Number: 2012907930

Printed in the United States of America

WestBow Press rev. date: 07/05/2012

CONTENTS

Resources

New King James Version
A Personal Study Bible for Holy Living
Copyright ©1990 by Thomas Nelson, Inc., Publishers

New American Standard Bible
Ryrie Study Bible Expanded Edition
Charles Caldwell Ryrie, Th.D., Ph.D.
Copyright © 1976, 1995 by Moody Press

The Hebrew-Greek Key Study Bible
New American Standard Bible
Copyright ©1984 and 1990 by AMG Publishers

VINE'S
Complete Expository Dictionary of Old and New Testament Words
W.E. Vine, Merrill F. Unger, William White, Jr.
A Personal Study Bible for Holy Living
Copyright © 1996 by Thomas Nelson, Inc., Publishers

Pocket Bible Handbook
An Abbreviated Bible Commentary
Henry H. Halley
Copyright © 1951, by Henry H. Halley

Christian Workers' Commentary on the Old and New Testaments
James M. Gray
Copyright © 1915, Fleming H. Revell Company

Training for the Ministry of Prayer Counseling
Basic and Advanced Manuals
John and Paula Sanford
Copyright © 1997
Elijah House, Inc.

Where To Find It in the Bible
Ken Anderson
Copyright © 1996 Ken Anderson
Publisher Thomas Nelson

ACKNOWLEDGMENTS

Joel Blakely first taught this study to the men's Sunday morning Bible study class at Westwood Baptist Mission so they would be able to walk in unity and hold steadfast to the truth learned together. Class members helped him to sharpen his skills as a teacher by questioning and sharing knowledge and experience, encouraging and blessing Joel as their teacher.

We want to dedicate this book to the class members: Arthur, Charles, Peter, Joe Lewis, Randy, and others who were there for a time. Thank you to each of you for your help in developing this study, and thank you for your obedience in being there and actively participating in the class, sharing what God has given you so this study came into being

Thank you also to those who have shared testimony and Scripture, those who read the original manuscript for error, and those who have encouraged and prayed as we worked through the process of bringing this work to publication. The excellent staff of Westbow Press has given us good measure running over. God has truly used their talents, dedication and abilities to help The 11:45 Call to "become".

It is our prayer that God will bless and prosper the work of these hands so lives may be changed and the work of the kingdom may be carried out according to God's plan.

PREFACE

We, Joel and Brenda Blakely, as laymen in the church, diligently sought to follow God as He showed us verse by verse and word by word how to put *The 11:45 Call* together in an expository Bible study. Teachers and professors had given us a foundation of study in the Bible. But God's Word is deep, and there is not enough time in a lifetime to have a full grasp of all it says.

When this task was undertaken, we recognized our limitations. However, we worked in the knowledge that God is bigger than either of us and capable of using what we bring to Him. Therefore, the development of the Bible studies God has led us to record has, by the necessity of our limitations, been completed with much prayer on our part and several requests for prayer support. God brought verses and text to us through sermons, calls from friends with a verse to share, our own devotion time, and random moments when God made His leading clear that what we were hearing was material to be recorded in this Bible study.

As this is being written, we all face a daily struggle to walk in the Light, confronted with evil that is at work all around us. It is not only ourselves but the whole of mankind that seems heavy pressed on every side. Our hearts break for those caught in or wandering into webs of deception and those who grope in the darkness waiting for the Light. We know we must bring this work forth so the readers will know of the hope that is within them.

Knowing that Jesus is the Light that we seek and holding a full appreciation for the value of God's Word, the Bible, we developed this study in the hopes that it would serve as a warning to a lost and dying world. It is our special hope that it would bring each of us into accountability and understanding of our responsibility to hold fast to the Truth as we live and teach by words, testimony, and/or the way we live our lives.

We have been blessed by friends and professors who took the time to teach us straight from the word of God. We are privileged to have people in our lives who encouraged and challenged us as we developed a Christian worldview as a filter for all we see and hear. Thank you to those who have taught us to rightly handle the word of God and held us accountable to be found faithful.

Those who have walked with and alongside us have been truthful with us when we erred in our walk with the LORD and in our service to His kingdom, have been diligent to speak with us, offering encouragement and insight. These faithful friends have prayed with us in bold honesty as they saw particular areas of our lives that needed prayer. We knew we were covered with prayer and concern as we have shared testimony and Scripture and taught classes.

A quick glance around us reveals preachers who "tickle" (2 Timothy 4:3 NAS) the ears of church attendees with their man-made doctrines. Motivational speeches that lack scriptural foundations are being expounded from the pulpit. New Age philosophies have crept into the church and caught many unawares. These teachings are replacing God's Word in preaching from the pulpit, Bible studies, and classrooms. The loss of focus is weakening (Mark 3:25) the "body" and creating confusion. Church leaders are building churches on doctrine that declare the word of God is in error. Even sexual immorality is being condoned from some church pulpits without respect for the clarity of God's laws and instructions regarding our bodies (1 Corinthians 3:16–17, 6:12–20).

We want to cry out to the world: "Stop, look, and listen." We hope this study will encourage you to pick up your copy of God's Word, the Bible, and read God's Words. God's Words are a call to the lost and instruction for the edification of the saints. Rightly handled (2 Timothy 2:15), these words will bring Truth to Light in your life and the lives of those around you. Let the work of God's Word and the

Holy Spirit renew your mind so you are able to live in the fullness of all God intended for you.

God has planned for you to be fitted for kingdom service. He has prepared garments of learning, protection, and sustenance for you to clothe and equip yourself for service (Ephesians 6:10–17) and provided His Word, the Bible, for instruction and the Holy Spirit to counsel and guide you as you learn and apply His lessons to your life (Romans 12:2). God knows your every need, and He knows what is ahead and behind you. Wherever you go, He is already there. He will walk every step of the way with you if you let Him.

God's Word is the Way, the Truth, and the Light, ancient words preserved for us to find our way. God's Word is life to sinners that were, in the first place, created for a purpose, to glorify our Father, God (1 Corinthians 6:20).

Joel first built this study to teach a group of men who were brought together in a street ministry mission. It was a diverse group from different cultures, backgrounds, and levels of understanding. Knowing that God brought them together for a reason and God had a plan, Joel prayerfully sought God's answer to the challenge of using appropriate material for teaching. He knew it must be material that would teach and effectively bring them into unity. Joel realized that the only thing that could unite and disciple this diverse group and prepare them for the work that God had planned was the direct word of God. So the next consideration was what book of the Bible to use first and how to present the study.

This is an expository study because we believe that the word of God is:

God breathed

> 2 Timothy 3:16 "All Scripture is given by inspiration of God, and is profitable for doctrine, for reproof, for correction, for instruction in righteousness."

Sharper than a two-edged sword

Hebrews 4:12 "For the word of God is living and powerful, and sharper than any two-edged sword, piercing even to the division of soul and spirit, and of joints and marrow, and is a discerner of the thoughts and intents of the heart."

Truth for the building up and edification of the saints

Ephesians 4:12–16 "For the equipping of the saints for the work of ministry, for the edifying of the body of Christ, [13]till we all come to the unity of the faith and of the knowledge of the Son of God, to a perfect man, to the measure of the stature of the fullness of Christ; [14]that we should no longer be children, tossed to and fro and carried about with every wind of doctrine, by the trickery of men, in the cunning craftiness of deceitful plotting, [15]but, speaking the truth in love, may grow up in all things into Him who is the head—Christ—[16]from whom the whole body, joined and knit together by what every joint supplies, according to the effective working by which every part does its share, causes growth of the body for the edifying of itself in love."

God's Word is alive and at work in those who hear and read it, just as it was in the days when Ezra read God's Word to the Israelites returning from Babylon. The reading/hearing of God's Word brought His people into the conviction of sin. The power of God's Word astonished Ezra.

Ezra 9:4 "Then everyone who trembled at the words of the God of Israel assembled to me, because of the transgression of those who had been carried away captive, and I sat astonished until the evening sacrifice."

With a keen sense of responsibility, we commit to bringing this work to reality for those who are called to read it. We believe the time is now to get our attention on the Word of God and lay aside the teaching of man. We believe time is of the essence. We teach because we believe it is important to encourage others and to help them understand that God has given us a call in His word that we may understand what is required of us (Micah 6:8) before the coming of the day of the LORD (Joel 2:28–32, Acts 2:17–21, 1 Thessalonians 5:2).

The midnight hour (Matthew 25:1–13) when we shall be going home is fast approaching. It is time to "awaken from sleep" (Romans 13:11, 1 Thessalonians5:4–6), be alert (Matthew 24:42), and "being sent out the midst of wolves . . . be wise as serpents and harmless as doves" (Matthew 10:16). God has issued *The 11:45 Call*, warning us the midnight hour and day of judgment will come.

INTRODUCTION

Jude, a half-brother of Jesus, walked and talked with Jesus. His writing is very similar to Peter's. God called each of these authors of a book of the Bible to pay attention to the leaven that was at work within the Church. God gave them each a burden for the dangers of the false teaching (2 Peter 2) that was working within the church to bring confusion and disruption. They were keenly aware of the threat, especially to those who were caught unawares, as the church was being confronted from within and not from the outside, as was expected.

The areas of danger Jude warns us about can overtake us, distract us, and confuse us. They are part of the enemy's plan to focus our attention toward himself and turn us away from our Creator. Jude encourages us to beware of false teaching. He alerts us to our call to study the word of God so we may be able to discern the truth (2 Timothy 2:14–28) and handle life circumstances circumspectly in such a manner as to please and honor God. Jude encourages us to build upon the foundation of Jesus Christ, God's son. Jesus gave His life so we may live in freedom and walk without falling.

Jude knew that Jesus, the Light of the World, would expose evil deeds and bring the Truth to Light (John 3:19–21) so the readers of Jude would be prepared for the day of Jesus's return.

Jesus's disciples asked Him, "Tell us, when will these things be? And what will be the sign of Your coming, and of the end of the age" (Matthew 24:3–4). Jude echoes the instructions of Jesus (Matthew 24:5) to His disciples. Jude instructs us to beware, be ready, and walk in faith, lifting high the cross of Christ and testifying to the work God has done in our lives. *The 11:45 Call* is the last call before judgment day.

EXPOSITORY BIBLE STUDY EXPLAINED

An expository Bible study of the book of Jude could give us the answers we seek to live in this perilous time. In biblical order, the book is placed just before Revelation, which may be God's way of telling us that the book of Jude is in place to prepare us for the Revelation times. This study is intended to explore the truths God gave us in the book of Jude so we might be prepared and able to stand alert and ready for God's call to His children to live out a serious faith.

According to Cooper P. Abrams III's *Principles of Literal Bible Interpretation*, the expository literal Bible study method uses scripture to interpret Scripture. When man interprets Scripture, our human nature tends to adjust the Scripture to fit his or her thought and need. This is not always intentional. It happens because man's sin nature flaws his mind. Therefore, man is not reliable to interpret the Scriptures on his own.

Revelation 22:18–19 tells us there are consequences for adding to or taking away from the words of the Bible. It is difficult for man to hold fast to the Truth. But it is possible with God's help (Matthew 19:26) and when our life (John 6:63) and mind are stayed upon Him (Isaiah 26:3) so the work of the Holy Spirit is manifested in all we do.

The mind of God is perfect and steadfast, and He is the Truth that we seek. Therefore, the word of God must interpret itself to be reliable. Second Timothy 3:16–17 tells us that all scripture is inspired by God and is profitable for equipping man for every good work.

We chose the expository literal-grammatical-historical method of Bible study because it does not rely on the wisdom of man but uses syntax, the study of the word in its grammatical and historical setting, to recognize the process of revelation (Abrams).

We tried several formats commonly available and finally decided that, for our initial audience, we would have to do something different. Therefore, this method of Bible study seeks to answer the following questions: who (man/God and the relationship of man to God), where (location), what (context, message, instruction, or thought), when (time and history), and how (application).

This study method we developed looks for principles of fundamental truth that are stated and restated so readers may determine how these principles apply to themselves, their life, the present age, and those around them. The learner is to determine what instructions are to accompany the principle. This method is a particularly effective way of equipping laymen.

Before you embark upon this study, ask yourself: Is Jude the 11:45 call? Is there special significance in the placement of the book of Jude right before the book of Revelation?

This study looks at the book of Jude in the context of the whole Bible so the reader/learner may be able to apply its principles to his or her life, turn from the confusion of the world, and find hope and help to live a godly life. Christians need a focal point so they may be empowered to conduct their lives in such a manner that the world would recognize them as followers of Christ. This study is written in the hope that it will serve as that focal point.

As you begin this study, pull out your copy of God's Word and, with prayer, ask God to help you to focus upon the Truth.

VERSE 1

"Jude, a bondservant of Jesus Christ and brother of James, to those who are called, sanctified by God the Father and preserved in Jesus Christ"

The author is Jude, a half-brother of Christ, a son of Joseph and Mary who was born after Jesus. The term "servant" would be fitting because of Jude's willingness to serve in the work that Jesus began and led. Jude could have claimed the honor of kinship to the Savior of the world, but Jude chose to serve with a humble attitude. At first, Jesus's brothers did not believe in Him. "For even HIS brothers did not believe Him" (John 7:5). Yet later, they saw the resurrected Christ and were convinced (Luke 24).

"These all continued with one accord in prayer and supplication, with the women and Mary, the mother of Jesus and with His brothers" (Acts 1:14). Among these was Jude/Judas, who did not consider himself worthy to call himself a brother but just a servant of Jesus Christ.

But God knew what He had planned for Jude. He knew who would be the mother and father and brothers and sisters of Jude. It was God's plan to place His unique creation, Jude, in the family of Jesus so everything in Jude's life prepared him for the task God planned for him to accomplish.

Bondservant

A bondservant is something much more meaningful than a slave. A bondservant is a willing slave. Exodus 21:1–6 explains a bondservant under the Mosaic Law as being, "one who gives himself up to another's will." Christ uses the service of bondservants in extending and advancing His cause among men. Jesus chose these men to carry out His work because of their devotion to another and the sharing of the gospel. Their work for the kingdom of God was done to the disregard of their own interests. They were committed to serve, willingly and wholeheartedly. This was the universal attitude of the apostles Paul, Titus, Peter, and James.

It is our calling as Christians to have this mind-set toward the LORD Jesus, willingly calling him "LORD" and serving Him as his bondservants. He set the example. He who had everything gave it all up, left His heavenly home, and came to earth to serve His Father.

> Philippians 2:7 "But made Himself of no reputation, taking the form of a bondservant, and coming in the likeness of men."

Of Jesus Christ

Jesus, the Greek form of the Hebrew name Joshua, means "salvation of Jehovah." The Savior of the world's name literally means salvation. Christ is not part of Jesus's name, but rather, it is a title meaning "the anointed one."

When Jude identifies Jesus as the Christ, he sets Him apart from and above all other deliverers, kings, or religious leaders. Jude says he willingly serves Jesus as a bondservant. Jude encourages us neither to overlook nor to underestimate the complete uniqueness of Jesus Christ, the one and only Son of God who is fully God and was fully man. Jude urges us to consider our service as bondservants to Jesus Christ.

And Brother of James

Jude identifies himself as the brother of the apostle James, who authored the epistle of James and is another half-brother of Jesus. James is another of the children born to Mary after Jesus' birth.

Mark 3:32 "And a multitude was sitting around Him; and they said to Him, "Look, Your mother and Your brothers are outside seeking You.""

Mark 6:3 "Is this not the carpenter, the Son of Mary, and brother of James, Joses, Judas, and Simon? And are not His sisters here with us?" So they were offended at Him."

Galatians 1:19 "But I saw none of the other apostles except James, the LORD's brother."

Matthew 13:55 "Is this not the carpenter's son? Is not His mother called Mary? And His brothers James, Joses, Simon, and Judas?"

Jude's Hebrew name was Judas.

To those who are called

This is another definition of a true Christian. God calls all Christians. The term "called" refers to both being "called out" of the world system and its priorities and to being "called to" God's purposes and plans.

Romans 1:7 "To all who are in Rome, beloved of God, called to be saints."

Romans 8:28 "And we know that all things work together for good to those who love God, to those who are the called according to His purpose."

1 Corinthians 1:2, "To the church of God, which is at Corinth, to those who are sanctified in Christ Jesus, called to be saints, with all who in every place call on the name of Jesus Christ our LORD, both theirs and ours:"

> 1 Corinthians 1:24, 26 "but to those who are called, both Jews and Greeks, Christ the power of God and the wisdom of God . . . [26]For you see your calling, brethren, that not many wise according to the flesh, not many mighty, not many noble, *are called*."

Sanctified ~Beloved~

This means purified and set apart for God, an essential part of being a Christian.

> 1 Corinthians 1:2, 30 "To the church of God which is at Corinth, to those who are sanctified in Christ Jesus, called to be saints, with all who in every place call on the name of Jesus Christ our LORD, both theirs and ours: [30]But of Him you are in Christ Jesus, who became for us wisdom from God—and righteousness and sanctification and redemption."

> Romans 15:16 "That I might be a minister of Jesus Christ to the Gentiles, ministering the gospel of God, that the offering of the Gentiles might be acceptable, sanctified by the Holy Spirit."

> 1 Thessalonians 4:3 "For this is the will of God; your sanctification, that you should abstain from sexual immorality."

By God the Father

A key characteristic of God is that He is "the Father." He is the Father of all things because He is the Creator. But He is also "God, the Father," identifying Him as distinct from "God, the Son, and God, the Holy Spirit."

Ephesians 4:6 "One God and Father of all, who is above all, and through all, and in you all."

John 10:30 (Jesus speaking) "I and My Father are one."

John 16:23 (Jesus speaking) "And in that day you will ask Me nothing. Most assuredly, I say to you, whatever you ask the Father in My name He will give you."

Our calling is not a result of any work of religion, denomination, other person(s), or the self. It is the work of God and God alone.

And preserved kept

Being preserved (kept, guarded, and protected) is necessary because of our natural human tendency to forget and to wander. We are born into the kingdom of God called, saved from eternal damnation, and sanctified. In order for us to grow, mature, and bear fruit this work of being called and saved that must be preserved, Jesus Christ guards and keeps watch over the souls He saves so we do not perish but will have everlasting life. Jesus assures us of our preservation.

John 10:29 (Jesus speaking) "My Father, who has given them to Me, is greater than all; and no one is able to snatch them out of My Father's hand."

John 6:37–40 (Jesus speaking) "All that the Father gives Me will come to Me, and the one who comes to Me I will by no means cast out. [38]For I have come down from heaven, not to do My own will, but the will of Him who sent Me. [39]This is the will of the Father who sent Me, that of all He has given Me I should lose nothing, but should raise it up at the last day. [40]And this is the will of Him who sent Me, that

5

> everyone who sees the Son and believes in Him may have everlasting life; and I will raise him up at the last day."

Jesus, the Good Shepherd, knows how to preserve His sheep.

> John 10:11 "I am the good shepherd. The good shepherd gives his life for the sheep."

In order to preserve the life and usefulness of a lamb that continually wanders from the flock, a shepherd may break the leg of the wandering lamb and carry that lamb around his neck until its leg heals. This makes the lamb totally dependent on the shepherd. For some lambs, this may be the only way they can be saved.

Paul assures the Philippians of the preservation of God's work in them.

> Philippians 1:6 "being confident of this very thing, that He who has begun a good work in you will complete it until the day of Jesus Christ."

In Jesus Christ

This means preserved "in Jesus Christ" as a called and sanctified person. The only true relationship with God is "in Jesus Christ."

Life Application Questions

- What characteristics of a bondservant does Jude demonstrate as he opens the writing of this book?
- Do you see the characteristics of bondservant in your own life?
- What made Jude recognize Jesus as God's son and Savior of the world?
- What does being called, saved, sanctified, and preserved mean to you?
- Has God called you into a true relationship with Him?

6

Verse 2

"Mercy, peace, and love be multiplied to you."

Mercy

This means compassion, kindness, and goodwill, especially in regard to judgment. Paul tells Timothy of the mercy he obtained.

> I Timothy 1:2, 13, 16 "To Timothy, a true son in the faith: grace, mercy, and peace from God our Father and Jesus Christ our LORD . . . . ¹³although I was formerly a blasphemer, a persecutor, and an insolent man; but I obtained mercy because I did it ignorantly in unbelief . . . . ¹⁶However, for this reason I obtained mercy, that in me first Jesus Christ might show all longsuffering, as a pattern to those who are going to believe on Him for everlasting life."

God tells Jeremiah to speak to His people, telling them that God will show mercy.

> Jeremiah 33:26 "Then I will cast away the descendants of Jacob and David My servant, so that I will not take any of his descendants to be rulers over the descendants of Abraham, Isaac, and Jacob. For I will cause their captives to return, and will have mercy on them."

The writer of Hebrew tells us to come to God to obtain mercy in a time of need.

> Hebrews 4:16 "Let us therefore come boldly to the throne
> of grace, that we may obtain mercy and find grace to help
> in time of need."

In Paul's letter to Titus, Paul explains that it is not by our righteousness that we are saved, but it is according to God's mercy.

> Titus 3:5 "Not by works of righteousness which we have
> done, but according to His mercy He saved us, through the
> washing of regeneration and renewing of the Holy Spirit."

Peter writes to tell us how God in His mercy took sinners and made them a people of God.

> 1 Peter 2:10 "Who once were not a people but are now the
> people of God, who had not obtained mercy but now have
> obtained mercy."

Peace

Peace is a security of mind and absence of fear of adversity. James encourages us to not just wish someone well who may have extra or special needs, but to go the extra mile and profit the kingdom of God so this person may truly be able to depart in peace.

> James 2:16 "And one of you says to them, "Depart in peace,
> be warmed and filled," but you do not give them the things
> which are needed for the body, what does it profit?"

Jesus is teaching His disciples. This verse comes after He spoke to them of the promise of help by the indwelling of the Holy Spirit. He gives them His peace to sustain them in the days ahead.

> John 14:27 (Jesus speaking) "Peace I leave with you, My peace I give to you; not as the world gives do I give to you. Let not your heart be troubled, neither let it be afraid."

The angels proclaim the peace on Earth that came with the birth of Jesus, the Christ child.

> Luke 2:14 "Glory to God in the highest, and on earth peace, goodwill toward men!"

Paul warns Timothy to flee youthful lusts and pursue the blessing of God.

> 2 Timothy 2:22 "Flee also youthful lusts; but pursue righteousness, faith, love, peace with those who call on the LORD out of a pure heart."

Paul provides a personal benediction of peace for the Thessalonians.

> 2 Thessalonians 3:16 "Now may the LORD of peace Himself give you peace always in every way. The LORD be with you all."

A salutation of grace, mercy, and peace are a part of Paul's letter to Titus.

> Titus 1:4 "To Titus, a true son in our common faith: grace, mercy, and peace from God the Father and the LORD Jesus Christ our Savior."

The faithful of the Old Testament believed and acted in faith and peace, including even Rahab.

Hebrews 11:31 "By faith the harlot Rahab did not perish with those who did not believe, when she had received the spies with peace."

Isaiah 26:3 "You will keep him in perfect peace, whose mind is stayed on you, because he trusts in you."

And love

This is the Greek word *agape* (*ag-ah'-pay*). It refers to the selfless, enduring love of God rather than the very limited love of mankind. The LORD maintains love and forgives sin. Paul instructs the Colossians regarding love (agape) and peace.

Colossians 3:14–15 "But above all these things put on love, which is the bond of perfection. ¹⁵And let the peace of God rule in your hearts."

Paul knew the Corinthians were going to need to have a better understanding of love (agape) if they were to carry out the work God had planned for them.

1 Corinthians 13 "Though I speak with the tongues of men and of angels, but have not love, I have become sounding brass or a clanging cymbal. ²And though I have the gift of prophecy, and understand all mysteries and all knowledge, and though I have all faith, so that I could remove mountains, but have not love, I am nothing. ³And though I bestow all my goods to feed the poor, and though I give my body to be burned, but have not love, it profits me nothing. ⁴Love suffers long and is kind; love does not envy; love does not parade itself, is not puffed up; ⁵does not behave rudely, does not seek its own, is not provoked, thinks no evil; ⁶does not rejoice in iniquity, but rejoices in the truth; ⁷bears all things,

believes all things, hopes all things, endures all things. [8]Love never fails. But whether there are prophecies, they will fail; whether there are tongues, they will cease; whether there is knowledge, it will vanish away. [9]For we know in part and we prophesy in part. [10]But when that which is perfect has come, then that which is in part will be done away. [11]When I was a child, I spoke as a child, I understood as a child, I thought as a child; but when I became a man, I put away childish things. [12]For now we see in a mirror, dimly, but then face to face. Now I know in part, but then I shall know just as I also am known. [13]And now abide faith, hope, love, these three; but the greatest of these is love."

Be multiplied to you

Jude is pronouncing a blessing of more than just mercy, peace, and love. He wishes a great multiplication of the mercy, peace, and love of God toward his readers. Jude is saying, "May these things both be present and continually increase toward you."

Life Application Questions

- How has God's mercy affected your life?
- Has any person ever shown you mercy?
- Do you know and understand the peace of God?
- How can you find "perfect peace"?
- Has there ever been a time in your life that you experienced God's peace in a difficult circumstance?
- Has the love of God had an impact on your life?
- How do you share the love of God with others?

Verse 3

"Beloved, while I was very diligent to write to you concerning our common salvation, I found it necessary to write to you exhorting you to contend earnestly for the faith which was once for all delivered to the saints."

Beloved

Agapetos (*ag-ap-ay-tos*) is a Greek word used to express godly intimacy and enduring love.

God used the same word to express His love for His Son in Matthew 3:17 when God said, "This is my beloved Son, in whom I am well pleased."

While I was very diligent to write to you

Jude is expressing his original desire to write this letter for the edification of his readers (the "you" he addresses this to). There seems to be a sense of eagerness in His desire to write and act on his responsibility to carry out God's work.

Concerning our common salvation

Jude originally intended to write about this topic. "Our common salvation" refers to the one thing all true Christians have in common, salvation.

To experience salvation is to be forgiven and delivered from the power and consequences of sin. The one thing all true Christians have in common is that they have received the gift of forgiveness of sins and the promise of eternal life in heaven with our heavenly Father, provided through the death, burial, and resurrection of Jesus Christ.

I found it necessary to write to you exhorting you to contend earnestly for the faith

Jude's original intention to write about our common salvation was changed as the Holy Spirit began working and prompting him to deal with a pressing issue "to contend earnestly for the faith."

This is an example for us, to be open to the leading of the Holy Spirit. As a child of God, you may have a very important and significant issue you wish to address. But the Holy Spirit may have a more important and more significant issue that needs immediate addressing. We are called to be open to His leading.

Exhorting

This means to urge and make an appeal. This same Greek word is "beseech."

> Romans 12:1 "I beseech you therefore brethren, by the mercies of God, that you present you bodies a living sacrifice, holy, acceptable to God, which is your reasonable service."

This same Greek word is "beg."

> Romans 15:30 "Now I beg you, brethren, through the Lord Jesus Christ, and through the love of the Spirit, that you strive together with me in prayers to God for me."

Contend earnestly

These two English words, "contend earnestly," actually come from one Greek word, *Epagonizomai*, meaning to fight continuously, to defend the faith (Truth). Until the LORD returns, the battle for the true faith will continue, and we are called to remain faithful to do whatever it takes to hold fast to that which is righteous.

The fight and the defense are both personal and corporate. Our personal fight is to hold fast to that which God commands and follow our calling. Corporately we are called to defend the faith and remain pure and undefiled. This means we are to prepare (Ephesians 6:10–17) and to persevere. We choose whether we want right things in our lives or not, and then we must contend earnestly to choose the right way.

God has provided a way for us as weak human beings, subject to follow our human nature, to gain the victory in this fight and remain steadfast. At the moment of salvation, the Holy Spirit comes to dwell within God's children to guide them through the battlefield each and every moment of their lives here on earth.

> John 16:13 "However, when He, the Spirit of truth, has come, He will guide you into all truth; for He will not speak on His own authority, but whatever He hears He will speak; and He will tell you things to come."

> Romans 8:26 "Likewise the Spirit also helps in our weaknesses. For we do not know what we should pray for as we ought, but the Spirit Himself makes intercession for us with groanings which cannot be uttered."

> Jude 20 "But you beloved, building yourselves up on your most holy faith, praying in the Holy Spirit."

You have available the whole armor of God as you face the fight, "contend earnestly," as you defend the Truth against the powers of darkness.

> Ephesians 6:12–13 "For we do not wrestle against flesh and blood, but against principalities, against powers, against the

rulers of the darkness of this age, against spiritual hosts of wickedness in the heavenly places. [13]Therefore take up the whole armor of God, that you may be able to withstand in the evil day, and having done all, to stand."

The armor is provided for your protection. Each individual has the choice to put it on or face the battle in his or her own strength and power.

The powers of darkness are superhuman but not all powerful. Their power fades in the Light of the power of the Holy Spirit. With the help of the Holy Spirit, you will be able to carry out God's work.

> Acts 1:8 (Jesus speaking) "But you shall receive power when the Holy Spirit has come upon you: and you shall be witnesses to Me in Jerusalem, and in all Judea and Samaria, and to the end of the earth."

God is more than able to handle the worldly battles and temptations that rob and plunder you and me.

> Isaiah 17:13–14 "The nations will rush like the rushing of many waters; But God will rebuke them and they will flee far away, And be chased like the chaff before the wind, Like a rolling thing before the whirlwind. [14]Then behold, at eventide, trouble! And before the morning, he is no more. This is the portion of those who plunder us, And the lot of those who rob us."

His power even works within the man or woman (the inner man) who submits and surrenders his or her all, everything he or she is and is not, to the LORD.

> Ephesians 3:16–17, 20 "that He would grant you, according to the riches of his glory, to be strengthened with might through His Spirit in the inner man [17]that Christ may

dwell in your heart through faith that you, being rooted and grounded in love . . . . [20]Now to Him who is able to do exceedingly abundantly above all the we ask or think, according to the power that works in us."

2 Corinthians 4:16 "Therefore we do not lose heart. Even though the outward man is perishing, yet the inward man is being renewed day by day."

The corporate battle against the powers of darkness belongs to the LORD. Scriptural examples include the time when a great multitude threatened Judah. (See 2 Chronicles 20 for the entire story.) Their leader, Jehoshaphat, led Judah to believe in the LORD and give the battle over to Him.

2 Chronicles 20:15 "And he said, Listen, all you of Judah and you inhabitants of Jerusalem, and you, King Jehoshaphat! Thus says the LORD to you: Do not be afraid nor dismayed because of this great multitude for the battle is not yours, but God's."

They obeyed, and God brought the victory.

2 Chronicles 20:22 "Now when they began to sing and to praise, the LORD set ambushes against the people of Ammon, Moab and Mount Seir, who had come against Judah; and they were defeated."

In a renewal of the Philistine invasion upon Israel, Goliath, the Philistine giant who stood a little over nine feet, challenged Israel to choose a person to face him. David, a young shepherd boy, stepped up and said, "Your servant will go and fight with this Philistine (1 Samuel 17:32). The Philistines were strong in battle. David stepped up to face Goliath, knowing he had no chance against Goliath. But he knew the

God he served was able. Goliath wore armor that weighed over 150 pounds and carried a spear that was over twenty pounds. David was victorious with just a slingshot and the armor of God.

> 1 Samuel 17:45, 50 "Then David said to the Philistine, You come to me with a sword, with a spear, and with a javelin. But I come to you in the name of the LORD of hosts, the God of the armies of Israel, who you have defied . . . [50]So David prevailed over the Philistine with a sling and a stone, and struck the Philistine and killed him. But there was no sword in the hand of David."

David "contended earnestly" by being prepared, seeking God, and showing up.

> 1 Samuel 17:47 "Then all the assembly shall know that the LORD does not save with sword and spear; for the battle is the LORD's and He will give you into our hands." (See the entire story in 1 Samuel 17.)

We are called, like Judah and David, to execute God's battle strategy, seek God, show up, and do all we are able to *contend earnestly* for the faith.

> 1 John 5:4 "For whatever is born of God overcomes the world. And this is the victory that has overcome the world—our faith."

When we surrender each of our enemies—Satan, the world, and self—to God, victory rises.

The faith

The true hope centers on the salvation through the gospel of Jesus Christ as described in the Scriptures. Faith is the indwelling of Christ—the

Way, the Truth, and the Life (John 14:6)—in us so we might be rooted and grounded in the Truth, know the love of Christ, and be filled with all the fullness of God.

> Ephesians 3:17–19 "that Christ may dwell in your hearts through faith; that you, being rooted and grounded in love [18]may be able to comprehend with all the saints what is the width and length and depth and height—[19]to know the love of Christ which passes knowledge; that you may be filled with all the fullness of God."

Faith is the victory that overcomes the world.

> 1 John 5:4–5 "For whatever is born of God overcomes the world. And this is the victory that has overcome the world—our faith."

As we face the battles, we are to take up the shield of faith.

> Ephesians 6:16 "above all, taking up the shield of faith with which you will be able to quench all the fiery darts of the wicked one."

Paul instructs the Christians at Philippi about the worthy conduct and a steadfast faith that both God and Paul expected from them.

> Philippians 1:27 "only let your conduct be worthy of the gospel of Christ, so that whether I come and see our or am absent, I may hear of your affairs, that you stand fast in one spirit, worth one mind striving together for the faith of the gospel."

Scripture gives us examples—Gideon (Judges. 7) and Joshua (Joshua 5:13–15, 6:1–27)—who were just two of the leaders who won victory by faith demonstrated by obedience.

Which was once for all delivered to the saints

The truth of the Gospel is permanent and unalterable, once for all delivered. God doesn't issue periodic revisions or updates, as many of today's cults would have you believe. The word "saints" here simply refers to all of God's people who have been made holy by the blood of Jesus. The New Living Translation (NLT) puts it this way: "God gave this unchanging truth once for all time to his holy people." The Twentieth Century New Testament (TCNT) says "entrusted" (gave).

> Galatians 1:6–8 "I marvel that you are turning away so soon from Him who called you in the grace of Christ, to a different gospel, [7]which is not another; but there are some who trouble you and want to pervert the gospel of Christ. [8]But even if we, or an angel from heaven, preach any other gospel to you than what we have preached to you, let him be accursed."

Life Application Questions

* What does the "common salvation" mean? And how does it affect you?
* How do you carry out your personal battle strategy and contend earnestly for the faith?
* How does knowing that God's Word is "unchanging truth" affect you?
* What do you need to do to let God bring the victory in your life?

Verse 4

"For certain men have crept in unnoticed, who long ago were marked out for this condemnation, ungodly men, who turn the grace of our God into lewdness and deny the only Lord God and our Lord Jesus Christ."

For certain men have crept in unnoticed

One of Satan's most effective strategies to spoil the work of God is to sneak/creep in unnoticed, placing his workers in among the fellowship of true believers. This is done just as in the world of espionage; one country might send a spy or a double agent into the inner workings of the enemy's government. He is also known to use someone who has a long relationship in the fellowship but, because of weakness, is vulnerable to the enemy's wiles.

Even in the early days of Christianity, Paul sent a warning to the Philippians that Christ was not always preached from pure motives.

> Philippians 1:15–16 "Some indeed preach Christ even from envy and stife, and some also from goodwill [16]The former preach Christ from selfish ambition, not sincerely, supposing to add affliction to my chains;"

"All that glitters is not gold." Not everyone who has found a place of leadership and influence in the church is actually chosen by God and godly. Unfortunately, some are moles of Satan. Whatever a man says or does, compare/filter it through a Biblical worldview (a modern term for our view(s) based on values and our body of knowledge) and in the context of the entire Bible. Examine yourself and let God examine you. You do not want Satan to use you to weaken the body of believers.

Paul warned the Romans to beware. Some Jews appeared to have accepted the gospel but continued to live under the law and taught the early Christians that they must live under the law. In their unrighteousness, they refused to accept the whole counsel of God and did not accept or believe the grace of the gospel. They were causing confusion with this false teaching.

> Romans 1:18 "For the wrath of God is revealed from heaven against all ungodliness and unrighteousness of men, who suppress the truth in unrighteousness."

The Jews were the first people God worked through to prepare the entire human race for salvation and holy righteous living. They used this advantage to move into the church, believing that God not judge them because they were under the law. Professing to be wise, they taught the law, but they did not keep it.

> Romans 1:22–25 "Because although they knew God, they did not glorify him as God, nor were thankful, but became futile in their thoughts, and their foolish hearts were darkened. 22Professing to be wise, they became fools, 23and changed the glory of incorruptible God into an image made like corruptible man—and bird and four-footed animals and creeping thing. 24Therefore God also gave them up to uncleaness, in the lusts of their hearts, to dishonor their bodies among themselves 25who exchanged the truth of God for the lie, and worshiped and served the creature rather than the Creator, who is blessed forever. Amen."

By breaking the law, they professed to raise the law alone (without the mercy and grace given to us at the cross) as the standard. The Jews blasphemed the name of God and lost the profit and witness.

Romans 2:17, 23 "Indeed you are called a Jew and rest on the law and make your boast in God, . . . 23You who make your boast in the law, do you dishonor God through breaking the law? 24For the name of God is blasphemed among the Gentiles because of you, as it is written. 25For circumcision is indeed profitable if you keep the law; but if you are a breaker of the law, your circumcision has become uncircumcision . . . . 29but he is a Jew who in one inwardly; and circumcision is that of the heart in the Spirit, not in the letter; whose praise is not from men but from God."

Legalistic, ungodly teaching was a threat to the Colossians, as Paul warns them.

Colossians 2:8,18, 20 "Beware lest anyone cheat you through philosophy and empty deceit, according to the tradition of men, according to the basic principles of the world, and not according to Christ. 18Let no one cheat you of your reward, taking delight in false humility and worship of angels, intruding into those things which he has not seen, vainly puffed up by his fleshly mind, 20Therefore, if you died with Christ from the basic principles of the world, why, as though living in the world, do you subject yourselves to regulations,"

Colossians 3:1–6 "If then you were raised with Christ, seek those things which are above, where Christ is, sitting at the right hand of God. 2Set your mind on things above, not on things on the earth. 3For you died, and your life is hidden with Christ in God. 4When Christ who is our life appears, then you also will appear with Him in glory. 5Therefore put to death your members which are on the earth: fornication, uncleanness, passion, evil desire, and covetousness, which is idolatry. ⁶Because of these things the wrath of God is coming upon the sons of disobedience,"

Timothy, whom Paul called a true son of the faith, was also warned of those who would sneak in and teach false (ungodly) doctrine.

1 Timothy 1:4 "Nor give heed to fables and endless genealogies, which cause disputes rather than godly edification which is in faith."

The adversary was using the sinful ways of those in the fellowship and the situation of widows as an opportunity to turn some to himself.

1 Timothy 5:11–15 "But refuse the younger widows; for when they have begun to grow wanton against Christ, they desire to marry, ¹²having condemnation because they have cast off their first faith. ¹³And besides they learn to be idle, wandering about from house to house, and not only idle but also gossips and busybodies, saying things which they ought not. ¹⁴Therefore I desire that the younger widows marry, bear children, manage the house, give no opportunity to the adversary to speak reproachfully. ¹⁵For some have already turned aside after Satan."

Some in the church were making unreasonable demands for support and harassing the church body with continual nagging and babbling. Because of this, true believers were becoming weary of doing well. Timothy was given this warning.

1 Timothy 5:8 "But if anyone does not provide for his own, and especially for those of his household he has denied the faith and is worse than an unbeliever."

Timothy was to "contend earnestly" by guarding what was committed to his trust.

> 1 Timothy 6:20 "O Timothy! Guard what was committed to your trust, avoiding the profane and idle babblings and contradictions of what is falsely called knowledge,"

For further instructions to Timothy, read 1 Timothy 4:6–16. The Thessalonians were similarly warned. See 2 Thessalonians 3:6–16.

Who long ago were marked out for this condemnation

These men and women, who Satan used to work undercover in the church, are destined/marked out for judgment by God for their evil ways. Their conduct is a denial of the work of Jesus Christ, so they will face the eternal judgment of God if they do not repent, just as Judas Iscariot did. Judas Iscariot was remorseful, not repentant.

> John 6:70–71 "Jesus answered them, 'Did I not choose you, the twelve, and one of you is a devil?' [71]He spoke of Judas Iscariot, the son of Simon, for it was he who would betray Him, being one of the twelve."

> Romans 9:22 "What if God, wanting to show His wrath and to make His power known endured with much longsuffering the vessels of wrath prepared for destruction."

> Hebrews 10:26 "For if we sin willfully after we have received the knowledge of the truth, there no longer remains a sacrifice for sins."

Ungodly men

These are men without God or godly influence. Though these men may be masquerading as workers of Christ, in truth, they are ungodly men/ godless/completely without God. The Bible refers to men. Women were not recognized or even counted in the early days of Christianity. But this applies to both men and women.

Nabal, the husband of Abigail who later married David, is referred to as an ungodly man in some translations. His name means "wilt" or "failure," and he is also referred to as a fool and scoundrel.

> 1 Samuel 25:3, 17, 25 "The name of the man was Nabal, and the name of his wife Abigail. And she was a woman of good understanding and beautiful appearance; but the man was harsh and evil in his doings. He was of the house of Caleb . . . ¹⁷Now therefore, know and consider what you will do, for harm is determined against our master and against all his household. For he is such a scoundrel that one cannot speak to him . . . ²⁵'Please, let not my LORD regard this scoundrel Nabal. For as his name is, so is he: ᶠNabal is his name, and folly is with him! But I, your maidservant, did not see the young men of my LORD whom you sent."

Nabal's choices and actions (1 Samuel 25) caused him to be marked for condemnation. As we find him in this Scripture, he was enjoying a feast, although he had refused to supply David's men their needs even as they had protected him.

> 1 Samuel 25: 36–38 "Now Abigail went to Nabal, and there he was, holding a feast in his house, like the feast of a king. And Nabal's heart was merry within him, for he was very drunk; therefore she told him nothing, little or much, until morning light. ³⁷So it was, in the morning, when the wine had gone from Nabal, and his wife had told him these

things, that his heart died within him, and he became like a stone. ³⁸Then it happened, after about ten days, that the LORD struck Nabal, and he died."

He was too late in realizing how his choices had put him in danger and his godly wife's action had saved him. When the truth came to him, his heart died within him, and he turned to stone. (God gave him a measure of grace, about ten more days, maybe time for a change of heart) scripture just says, "The LORD struck Nabal, and he died."

Who turn the grace of our God into lewdness

Turning grace into lewdness are characteristics of ungodly men who have infiltrated the church ranks.

God's grace brings mercy and forgiveness through the work of Christ to cover repented sin.

> Ephesians 2:8 "For by grace you have been saved through faith, and that not of yourselves; *it is* the gift of God,"

> John 1:14–17 "And the Word became flesh and dwelt among us, and we beheld His glory, the glory as of the only begotten of the Father, full of grace and truth. ¹⁵John bore witness of Him and cried out, saying, 'This was He of whom I said, 'He who comes after me is preferred before me, for He was before me.' ¹⁶And of His fullness we have all received, and grace for grace. ¹⁷For the law was given through Moses, *but* grace and truth came through Jesus Christ."

> Matthew 4:17 "From that time on Jesus began to preach and to say, 'Repent for the kingdom of heaven is at hand.'"

Lewdness is unbridled lust and uncontrolled sinful living. These two words, grace and lewdness, are in direct opposition to each other.

This phrase would indicate that these men took advantage of God's grace and possibly even taught others to do so by living in sin that grace may be increased. False teaching mistakenly led people to think that continuing to sin, lewdness, was good because it gave an opportunity for a greater measure of God's grace to be applied to their lives, as if they were still under the law rather than the work of the cross and the New Covenant.

> Romans 6:11–14 "Likewise you also, reckon yourselves to be dead indeed to sin, but alive to God in Christ Jesus our LORD. ¹²Therefore do not let sin reign in your mortal body, that you should obey it in its lusts. ¹³And do not present your members as instruments of unrighteousness to sin, but present yourselves to God as being alive from the dead, and your members as instruments of righteousness to God. ¹⁴For sin shall not have dominion over you, for you are not under law but under grace."

The pagan Gentiles rejected God because of their darkened understanding and blind heart. And thus, in alienation from God, they gave themselves over to lewdness (lust and greed).

> Ephesians 4:18–19 "having their understanding darkened, being alienated from the life of God, because of the ignorance that is in them, because of the blindness of their heart: ¹⁹who being past feeling, have given themselves over to lewdness, to work all uncleanness with greediness."

Jude warns us not to imitate them. Gnostics believe knowledge is the most important part of religion. Gnostic heresy taught that it didn't matter what you did with your body since the body was utterly sinful anyway. This sort of thinking would promote an undisciplined lifestyle and loose immoral living, turning the grace of God into lewdness.

This word of God that came to Jeremiah regarding Judah's disgrace helps us to gain a better understanding of lewdness. It refers to Judah's refusal to be made clean before God. Because of their harlotry and abominations, God pronounces woe upon them.

> Jeremiah 13:27 "I have seen your adulteries And your lustful neighings, The lewdness of your harlotry, Your abominations on the hills in the fields. Woe to you, O Jerusalem! Will you still not be made clean?"

And deny the only LORD God and our LORD Jesus Christ

Deny is to refuse or be unable to believe or accept something. The word "LORD" is used twice in this short phrase in verse 4, even though these are two different words in Greek. The first is *despotes* (*des-pot'-ace*), meaning "ruler" or "master." This is the same Greek word Peter used in 2 Peter 2:1 for LORD (NKJ) and Master (NASB). The second is *kurios* (*koo'-ree-os*), a title of respect given to a master.

Both words for LORD are used in the New Testament with reference to both God and Jesus. The Greek manuscripts from which the newer translations come do not have the word "God" in this phrase and read like this:

> "deny our only Master and LORD, Jesus Christ" (NASB95/ New American Standard 1995).

Sinful conduct is a way of denying God's work in our lives and negates the power of God's work in our lives. Earlier in this verse, we are warned that to believe and teach that it is okay to live in sin turns the grace of God into "lewdness" and denies the LORDship of Christ in your life. To deny that Jesus is the Son of God is to break fellowship, deny the LORDship, with the Father. He who has the Father must know that the Father bought us by sending His Son that we might have eternal life.

1 John 2:22–23 "Who is a liar but he who denies that Jesus is the Christ? He is antichrist who denies the Father and the Son. ²³Whoever denies the Son does not have the Father either; he who acknowledges the Son has the Father also."

2 Peter 2:1 "But there were also false prophets among the people, even as there will be false teachers among you, who will secretly bring in destructive heresies, even denying the LORD who bought them and bring on themselves swift destruction."

Peter denies even knowing Jesus as Jesus was on trial.

Mark 14:72 "A second time the rooster crowed. Then Peter called to mind the work that Jesus had said to him. 'Before the rooster crows twice, you will deny Me three times.' And when he thought about it, he wept." (For more, see Mark 14:66–72, Matthew 26:69–75, Luke 22:56–62, and John 18:15–18, 25–28.)

Peter repented, and he was commissioned.

John 21:17 "He said to him the third time, (Jesus speaking) 'Simon, son of Jonah, do you love Me?' Peter was grieved because He said to him the third time, 'Do you love Me?' And he said to Him, 'LORD you know all things; You know that I love you.' Jesus said to him, 'Feed My sheep.'"

And God used Peter mightily in the work of God's kingdom.

Acts 2:37–39 "Now when they heard this, they were cut to the heart, and said to Peter and the rest of the apostles, 'Men and brethren, what shall we do?' ³⁸Then Peter said to them, 'Repent, and let every one of you be baptized in the name of

Jesus Christ for the remission of sins; and you shall receive the gift of the Holy Spirit. [39]For the promise is to you and to your children and to all who are afar off, as many as the LORD our God will call.'"

The one who has Jesus Christ as LORD and Master seeks to obey Christ's commands to live a holy life.

1 John 5:1–5 "Whoever believes that Jesus is the Christ is born of God, and everyone who loves Him who begot also loves him who is begotten of Him. [2]By this we know that we love the children of God, when we love God and keep His commandments. [3]For this is the love of God, that we keep His commandments. And His commandments are not burdensome. [4]For whatever is born of God overcomes the world. And this is the victory that has overcome the world—our faith. [5]Who is he who overcomes the world, but he who believes that Jesus is the Son of God?"

Life Application Questions

- In what areas of your life do you live as if it is okay to sin?
- How does this affect your testimony regarding Jesus as LORD and Master of your life?
- What can you do about it?
- What is the difference between being remorseful and being repentant?

VERSE 5

"But I want to remind you, though you once knew this, that the LORD, having saved the people out of the land of Egypt, afterward destroyed those who did not believe."

This is a warning from Jude that there are consequences for unbelief.

But I want to remind you, though you once knew this

Jude reminds you (readers of Jude) of this, God will hold you accountable. Christians must continue to read and study the Bible because we forget and we need reminding. God knows our every weakness. He knows that, as frail human beings, it is possible for us to have once known the Truth of God. Many of us have been taught from God's Word and/or heard testimony of God's faithfulness from parents or teachers. Or it may have even been just yesterday that we received instruction and Truth.

But our human nature is to wander from the Truth, to lose focus, to become distracted and/or caught up by worldly pursuits, and then to forget what God has done and given to us. As a reminder, Paul writes to the Romans.

> Romans 15:15 "Nevertheless, brethren, I have written more boldly to you on some points, as reminding you, because of the grace given to me by God,"

31

Peter also reminds his readers.

> 2 Peter 1:12–13 "For this reason I will not be negligent to remind you always of these things, though you know and are established in the present truth. [13]Yes, I think it is right, as long as I am in this tent, to stir you up by reminding you."

> 2 Peter 3:1. "Beloved, I now write you this second epistle (in both of which I stir up your pure minds by way of reminder)."

That the LORD, having saved the people out of the land of Egypt, afterward destroyed

In verse 5, Jude gives us the first of three examples (Verse 5: Israelites, Verse 6: fallen angels, and Verse 7: Sodom and Gomorrah) of people or beings who have turned from God's truth after having a full knowledge of the Truth and the consequences of unbelief and disobedience.

In the first example of God's expectation and judgment, Jude presents the famous story of the Exodus out of the land of Egypt. The very people who experienced such a great deliverance from the hands of Pharaoh in Egypt ended up destroyed/cast off and exiled in the wilderness by the same God who delivered them in the first place because they took matters into their own hands, worrying about themselves rather than trusting God. God was displeased at their dissatisfaction with what He provided for them.

> Numbers 11:1–6, 23 "Now when the people complained, it displeased the LORD; for the LORD heard it, and His anger was aroused. So the fire of the LORD burned among them, and consumed some in the outskirts of the camp. [2]Then the people cried out to Moses, and when Moses prayed to the LORD, the fire was quenched. [3]So he called the name of the place Taberah, because the fire of the LORD had burned

among them. [4]Now the mixed multitude who were among them yielded to intense craving; so the children of Israel also wept again and said: "Who will give us meat to eat? [5]We remember the fish which we ate freely in Egypt, the cucumbers, the melons, the leeks, the onions, and the garlic; [6]but now our whole being is dried up; there is nothing at all except this manna before our eyes!' . . . [23]And the LORD said to Moses, "Has the LORD's arm been shortened? Now you shall see whether what I say will happen to you or not."

The Israelites were dissatisfied with the leader God had given to them and reflected upon God's will by attacking his character. They were attacking a man God had put in place and God had shown favor. Moses walked so close to God that God even spoke to him face to face. God defended Moses, and when God had enough of their grumbling, He departed from their presence.

Numbers 12:1–9 "Then Miriam and Aaron spoke against Moses because of the Ethiopian woman whom he had married; for he had married an Ethiopian woman. [2]So they said, "Has the LORD indeed spoken only through Moses? Has He not spoken through us also?" And the LORD heard it. [3](Now the man Moses was very humble, more than all men who were on the face of the earth.) [4]Suddenly the LORD said to Moses, Aaron, and Miriam, "Come out, you three, to the tabernacle of meeting!" So the three came out. [5]Then the LORD came down in the pillar of cloud and stood in the door of the tabernacle, and called Aaron and Miriam. And they both went forward. [6]Then He said, "Hear now My words: If there is a prophet among you, I, the LORD, make Myself known to him in a vision; I speak to him in a dream. [7]Not so with My servant Moses; He is faithful in all My house. [8]I speak with him face to face, even plainly, and not in dark sayings; and he sees the form of the LORD. Why then were you not afraid to speak against My servant Moses?" ⁹So the anger of the LORD was aroused against them, and He departed."

God could have used the testimony of His people after their release from Egypt to glorify Himself. But because the people were complaining instead of praising, they tarnished their witness.

Numbers 14:1–17 "So all the congregation lifted up their voices and cried, and the people wept that night. ²And all the children of Israel complained against Moses and Aaron, and the whole congregation said to them, "If only we had died in the land of Egypt! Or if only we had died in this wilderness! ³Why has the LORD brought us to this land to fall by the sword, that our wives and children should become victims? Would it not be better for us to return to Egypt?" ⁴So they said to one another, "Let us select a leader and return to Egypt." ⁵Then Moses and Aaron fell on their faces before all the assembly of the congregation of the children of Israel. ⁶But Joshua the son of Nun and Caleb the son of Jephunneh, who were among those who had spied out the land, tore their clothes; ⁷and they spoke to all the congregation of the children of Israel, saying: "The land we passed through to spy out is an exceedingly good land. ⁸If the LORD delights in us, then He will bring us into this land and give it to us, 'a land which flows with milk and honey.' ⁹Only do not rebel against the LORD, nor fear the people of the land, for they are our bread; their protection has departed from them, and the LORD is with us. Do not fear them." ¹⁰And all the congregation said to stone them with stones. Now the glory of the LORD appeared in the tabernacle of meeting before all the children of Israel. ¹¹Then the LORD said to Moses: "How long will these people reject Me? And how long will they not believe Me, with all the signs which I have performed among them? [12]I will strike them with the pestilence and disinherit them, and I will make of you a nation greater and mightier than they." [13]And Moses said to the LORD: "Then the Egyptians will hear it, for by Your might You brought these people up from among them, [14]and they will tell it to the inhabitants of this land. They have heard that You, LORD, are among these people; that You, LORD, are seen face to face and Your cloud stands above them, and You go before them in a pillar of cloud by day and in a pillar of fire by night. [15]Now if You kill these people as one man, then the nations which have heard of Your fame will speak, saying, [16]'Because the LORD was not able to bring this people to the land which He swore to give them, therefore He killed them in the wilderness.' [17]And now, I pray, let the power of my LORD be great, just as You have spoken, saying,"

Numbers 14:22–37 "because all these men who have seen My glory and the signs which I did in Egypt and in the wilderness, and have put Me to the test now these ten times, and have not heeded My voice, [23]they certainly shall not see the land of which I swore to their fathers, nor shall any of those who rejected Me see it. [24]But My servant Caleb, because he has a different spirit in him and has followed Me fully, I will bring into the land where he went, and his descendants shall inherit it. [25]Now the Amalekites and the Canaanites dwell in the valley; tomorrow turn and move out into the wilderness by the Way of the Red Sea" [26]And the LORD spoke to Moses and Aaron, saying, [27]"How long shall I bear with this evil congregation who complain against Me? I have heard the complaints which the children of Israel make against Me. [28]Say to them, 'As I live,' says the LORD, 'just as you have spoken in My hearing, so I will do to you: [29]The carcasses of you who have complained against Me shall fall in this wilderness, all of you who were numbered, according to your entire number, from twenty years old and above. [30]Except for Caleb the son of Jephunneh and Joshua the son of Nun, you shall by no means enter the land which I swore I would make you dwell in. [31]But your little ones, whom you said would be victims, I will bring in, and they shall know the land which you have despised. [32]But as for you, your carcasses shall fall in this wilderness. [33]And your sons shall be shepherds in the wilderness forty years, and bear the brunt of your infidelity, until your carcasses are consumed in the wilderness. [34]According to the number of the days in which you spied out the land, forty days, for each day you shall bear your guilt one year, namely forty years, and you shall know My rejection. [35]I the LORD have spoken this. I will surely do so to all this evil congregation who are gathered together against Me. In this wilderness they shall be consumed, and there they shall die.'" [36]Now the men whom Moses sent to spy out the land, who returned and made all the congregation complain against him by bringing a bad report of the land, [37]those very men who brought the evil report about the land, died by the plague before the LORD."

Ten of those who were sent out to see the land God had promised to them viewed the land through human eyes and a mind that was not stayed upon God and His plan and vision for His children. They totally ignored the fact that God had already planned for them to be blessed. They broadcast their negative view and sought to bring others into their court. Their plan failed, and they experienced God's judgment, that is, died by the plague, for their lack of faith. They brought disaster upon themselves because they were fearful instead of faithful.

This example of the Israelites' wilderness experience (Desert U) is used repeatedly in the Scriptures. God is making His point.

Those who did not believe

Those who were sent out to spy out the land lacked belief in the power of God to overcome the giants they saw in the land where they had been sent as spies. Their foresight did not include the ability of God to provide what was needed for them to take possession of the land. They demonstrated their lack of faith and trust by complaining about God's ability to sustain them in the manner of which they deemed they were worthy, the manner they had experienced in Egypt. Their attitude of belief did not include God's sovereignty and omnipotence. They did not believe that God was able to handle their circumstances.

Unbelief brought destruction to the people of God after God had delivered them. They forgot what God had done in Egypt and times before and acted unfaithfully. By not seeing the abundance of fruit, milk, and honey that filled this fertile land, they missed the blessing and potential that God had planned for them to enjoy.

Only Caleb and Joshua had the ability (a different spirit, verse 24) to see the land that God had sent them to spy out. Caleb saw the land through God's eyes and God's ability to overcome the obstacles and problems they viewed, and he and Joshua received the favor of God.

> Romans 11:20–21 "Because of unbelief they were broken off, and you stand by faith. Do not be haughty, but fear. ²¹For God did not spare the natural branches. He may not spare you either."

> Hebrews 3:19 "So we see that they could not enter in because of unbelief."

> Psalm 78:52–57 "But He made His own people go forth like sheep, and guided them in the wilderness like a flock; ⁵³and He led them on safely, so that they did not fear; but the sea overwhelmed their enemies. ⁵⁴And He brought them to His holy border, this mountain which His right hand

had acquired. [55]He also drove out the nations before them, allotted them an inheritance by survey, and made the tribes of Israel dwell in their tents. [56]Yet they tested and provoked the Most High God, And did not keep His testimonies, [57]but turned back and acted unfaithfully like their fathers; they were turned aside like a deceitful bow."

In another effort to allow Israel to follow Him, the LORD gave Moses the second recording of the Ten Commandments. At this time, the LORD proclaimed to Moses:

> Exodus 34:6 "And the LORD passed before him and proclaimed, 'The LORD, the LORD God, merciful and gracious, longsuffering, and abounding in goodness and truth. [7]keeping mercy for thousands, forgiving iniquity and transgression and sin, by no means clearing the guilty, visiting the iniquity of the fathers upon the children and children's children to the third and the fourth generation.'"

Life Application Questions

- Why do you think God saved His people just to destroy them later?
- Is God the God of second chances?
- Think of an example from the Scriptures of God giving second chances.
- Why did God favor Caleb and Joshua and allow them to enter the Promised Land?
- What times in your life have you faced a seemingly impossible task just to find out that, when you committed it to God and trusted Him to lead the way and make provision, you had the privilege of witnessing the miracle of God's power at work? Or have you seen this happen to someone around you?

VERSE 6

"And the angels who did not keep their proper domain, but left their own abode, He has reserved in everlasting chains under darkness for the judgment of the great day;"

And the angels who did not keep their proper domain, but left their own abode

Jude illustrates his point. God will judge, and there are consequences (Hebrews 10:31) with a second example of turning from God's Truth, the fallen angels. Angels are beings that God created before the world was in place. Their domain was to surround the throne of God even before the world was created. Angels are mentioned numerous times in the Scriptures. Angels carry out God's work.

> Psalm 78:49 "He cast on them the fierceness of His anger, Wrath, indignation, and trouble, by sending angels of destruction among them."

> Psalm 103:20 "Bless the LORD, you His angels, who excel in strength, who do His word, heeding the voice of His word."

An angel set Peter free.

> Acts 12:7 "Now behold, an angel of the LORD stood by him, and a light shone in the prison; and he struck Peter on the side and raised him up, saying, 'Arise quickly!' And his chains fell off his hands."

And an angel struck Herod.

> Acts 12:23 "Then immediately an angel of the LORD struck him, because he did not give glory to God. And he was eaten by worms and died."

Angels deliver messages for God, such as the one delivered to Manoah's wife, Samson's mother.

> Judges 13:3, 6–7 "And the Angel of the LORD appeared to the woman and said to her, "Indeed now, you are barren and have borne no children, but you shall conceive and bear a son." ⁶So the woman came and told her husband, saying, "A Man of God came to me, and His countenance was like the countenance of the Angel of God, very awesome; but I did not ask Him where He was from, and He did not tell me His name. ⁷And He said to me, 'Behold, you shall conceive and bear a son. Now drink no wine or similar drink, nor eat anything unclean, for the child shall be a Nazirite to God from the womb to the day of his death.'"

Angels surround the throne of God.

> Revelation 5:11 "Then I looked, and I heard the voice of many angels around the throne, the living creatures, and the elders; and the number of them was ten thousand times ten thousand, and thousands of thousands."

Angels do not marry.

> Mark 12:25 (Jesus speaking) "For when they rise from the dead, they neither marry nor are given in marriage, but are like angels in heaven."

Manna, the bread of heaven, is angel food.

> Psalm 78:24–25 "Had rained down manna on them to eat, and given them of the bread of heaven. ²⁵Men ate angels' food; He sent them food to the full."

Angels deserve a worthy reception, such as the one Paul received.

> Galatians 4:14 "And my trial which was in my flesh you did not despise or reject, but you received me as an angel of God, even as Christ Jesus."

But we are not to worship angels.

> Colossians 2:18 "Let no one cheat you of your reward, taking delight in false humility and worship of angels, intruding into those things which he has not seen, vainly puffed up by his fleshly mind."

Man is a little lower than the angels. (Jesus came as a man.)

> Hebrews 2:9 "But we see Jesus, who was make a little lower than the angels, for the suffering of death crowned with glory and honor, that He, by the grace of God, might taste death for everyone."

Proper domain

This means the fitting territory of activity and place of abode. For angels, this is heaven. Angels in heaven always see the face of Father God.

> Matthew 18:10 (Jesus speaking) "Take heed that you do not despise one of these little ones, for I say to you that in

heaven their angels always see the face of My Father who is in heaven."

Angels on mission come down from heaven and do their work for God here on Earth.

> Revelation 10:1 "I saw still another mighty angel coming down from heaven, clothed with a cloud. And a rainbow was on his head, his face was like the sun, and his feet like pillars of fire."

> Luke 2:13–15 "And suddenly there was with the angel a multitude of the heavenly host praising God and saying: 14"Glory to God in the highest, and on earth peace, goodwill toward men!" 15So it was, when the angels had gone away from them into heaven, that the shepherds said to one another, "Let us now go to Bethlehem and see this thing that has come to pass, which the LORD has made known to us.""

God cast the Devil and his angels out of heaven, and they no longer saw the face of God or did his biding. Even angels face God's prepared judgment.

> Matthew 25:41 (Jesus speaking) "Then He will also say to those on the left hand, 'Depart from Me, you cursed, into the everlasting fire prepared for the devil and his angels.'"

There are just a few places in Scripture where we can read of the angels who rebelled or fell away from God.

> Isaiah 14:12–14 "How you are fallen from heaven, O Lucifer, son of the morning! How you are cut down to the ground, you who weakened the nations! 13For you have said in your heart: 'I will ascend into heaven, I will exalt my

throne above the stars of God; I will also sit on the mount of the congregation on the farthest sides of the north.' [14]I will ascend above the heights of the clouds, I will be like the Most High."

Satan, the dragon, drew away angels, the stars of heaven.

> Revelation 12:4 "His tail drew a third of the stars of heaven and threw them to the earth. And the dragon stood before the woman who was ready to give birth, to devour her Child as soon as it was born."

He has reserved in everlasting chains under darkness for the judgment of the great day

The fate of the fallen angels is very grave and grievous. He has reserved a place for judgment for the fallen angels.

> 2 Peter 2:4, 9 "For if God did not spare the angels who sinned, but cast them down to hell and delivered then into chains of darkness, to be reserved for judgment. . . . [9]Then the Lord knows how to deliver the godly out of temptations and to reserve the unjust under punishment for the day of judgment,"

Chains under darkness

Darkness (evil) that lasts forever and chains that cannot be loosened are reserved for eternal judgment. Unlike God's children, who have chosen to follow Him, the condemned are without hope of reprieve ever.

> Revelation 20:10–11 "The devil, who deceived them, was cast into the lake of fire and brimstone where the beast and the false prophet are. And they will be tormented day and

night forever and ever. ¹¹Then I saw a great white throne and Him who sat on it, from whose face the earth and the heaven fled away. And there was found no place for them."

Revelation 20:1 "Then I saw an angel coming down from heaven, having the key to the bottomless pit and a great chain in his hand."

Judgment of the great day

This is also called the day of the LORD.

2 Peter 3:10–13 "But the day of the LORD will come as a thief in the night, in which the heavens will pass away with a great noise, and the elements will melt with fervent heat; both the earth and the works that are in it will be burned up. ¹¹Therefore, since all these things will be dissolved, what manner of persons ought you to be in holy conduct and godliness, ¹²looking for and hastening the coming of the day of God, because of which the heavens will be dissolved, being on fire, and the elements will melt with fervent heat? ¹³Nevertheless we, according to His promise, look for new heavens and a new earth in which righteousness dwells."

Joel 3:13–17 "Put in the sickle, for the harvest is ripe. Come, go down; for the winepress is full, the vats overflow—for their wickedness is great." ¹⁴Multitudes, multitudes in the valley of decision! For the day of the LORD is near in the valley of decision. ¹⁵The sun and moon will grow dark, and the stars will diminish their brightness. ¹⁶The LORD also will roar from Zion, and utter His voice from Jerusalem; the heavens and earth will shake; but the LORD will be a shelter for His people, and the strength of the children of Israel. ¹⁷"So you shall know that I am the LORD your God,

dwelling in Zion My holy mountain. Then Jerusalem shall
be holy, and no aliens shall ever pass through her again."

The "valley of decision" here represents God's decision, not mankind
or the nations. God assures us that the demonic forces will be defeated
on the day of the LORD.

Life Application Questions

* What does it mean that the "angels did not keep their proper domain"?
* What are "chains under darkness"?
* Are you ready for judgment day? If not, what will you change in your life to be ready?

VERSE 7

"As Sodom and Gomorrah, and the cities around them in a similar manner to these, having given themselves over to sexual immorality and gone after strange flesh, are set forth as an example, suffering the vengeance of eternal fire."

As Sodom and Gomorrah, and the cities around them in a similar manner to these

Jude's third example of those who reject God's truth is the story of Sodom and Gomorrah, which you can read about in Genesis 10–19, as well as various references throughout the Scriptures.

Sodom and Gomorrah do not stand alone here. There are other references to the cities around them who were also living to satisfy the flesh rather than to please God and be used as an instrument of righteousness. The New American Standard Bible uses the word "indulged," meaning satisfying self and desire.

> Jude 7 "the cities around them, since they in the same way as these indulged in gross immorality and went after strange flesh, are exhibited as an example, in undergoing the punishment of eternal fire (NASB)."

> Deuteronomy 29:23 "the whole land is brimstone, salt, and burning; it is not sown, nor does it bear, nor does any grass grow there like the overthrow of Sodom and Gomorrah, Admah, and Zeboiim, which the LORD overthrew in His anger and His wrath."

Isaiah 13:19 "And Babylon, the glory of kingdom, the beauty of the Chaldeans' pride will be as when God overthrew Sodom and Gomorrah."

Sodom and Gomorrah are also mentioned in the following:

Jeremiah 49:18 "As in the overthrow of Sodom and Gomorrah and their neighbors," says the LORD, No one shall remain there, nor shall a son of man dwell in it."

Jeremiah 50:40 "As God overthrew Sodom and Gomorrah and their neighbors," says the LORD. So shall no one reside there, Nor son of man dwell in it."

Amos 4:11 "I overthrew *some* of you, as God overthrew Sodom and Gomorrah, and you were like a firebrand plucked from the burning; yet you have not returned to Me," says the LORD."

Luke 10:12 "But I say to you that it will be more tolerable in that Day for Sodom than for that city." (See Luke 10:1–12 for the entire story.)

For the story of judgment and destruction on Sodom and Gomorrah, read Genesis 18:16–19:29. Genesis 19:24–25 tells what happened to Sodom, Gomorrah, and the cities around them.

Genesis 19:24–25 "Then the LORD rained brimstone and fire on Sodom and Gomorrah, from the LORD out of the heavens. [25]So He overthrew those cities, all the plain, all the inhabitants of the cities and what grew on the ground."

Having given themselves over to sexual immorality and gone after strange flesh

The New American Standard uses the words "gone after," indicating they pursued immorality and strange flesh. Strange flesh means unnatural or homosexual abominations, that is, carnal.

> Romans 1:27 "Likewise also the men, leaving the natural use of the woman, burned in their lust for one another, men with men committing what is shameful, and receiving in themselves the penalty of their error which was due."

> Genesis 19:5 "And they called to Lot and said to him, where are men [the two angels who came to Lot in 19:1] who came to you tonight? Bring them out to us that we may know them carnally."

Carnally means have homosexual intercourse. This is to rebel against or deny God's plan for intercourse between a man and a woman and to miss the fullness and beauty of God's plan.

Those in Sodom also indulged in other lusts of the flesh

Lusts of the flesh, that is, satisfying ourselves, are an abomination to God, and He deals with this iniquity (sin) as He sees fit.

> Ezekiel 16:49–50 "Look, this was the iniquity of your sister Sodom: She and her daughter had pride, fullness of food, and abundance of idleness; neither did she strengthen the hand of the poor and needy. 50And they were haughty and committed abomination before Me; therefore I took them away as I saw fit."

Are set forth as an example, suffering the vengeance of eternal fire

Those in Sodom were set forth as an example to God's people of the wrongdoing of the false prophets and those who mislead God's people. These wrongdoers will face the judgment of God upon those people.

Jude warns his readers by explaining what was happening. The false teachers of his day were trying to lead the people of Jude's time into the same immorality that brought judgment, the vengeance of eternal fire, upon Sodom and Gomorrah.

Vengeance is punishment in return for wrongdoing. Eternal fire is what many refer to as hellfire, where there will be weeping and gnashing of teeth as they experience the eternal horrors of judgment.

Hellfire is mentioned in Matthew 5, where Jesus explains God's kind of righteousness and judgment of sins. A person is to get right with God even when there has already been judgment by a human court or counsel. The human court or counsel may not even be aware of the hidden sin, which only God knows and judges. God knows the heart.

> Matthew 5:22 "But I say to you that whoever is angry with his brother without a cause shall be in danger of the judgment and whoever says to his brother Raca! Shall be in danger of the council. But whoever says, You fool! Shall be in danger of hell fire."

Raca, an Aramaic word, means "empty." This term is used as one of contempt. To say this was worse than being angry. It was an outrageous utterance. Using the term in anger without cause toward one's brother would put one in danger of hell fire. In Judges 9:4, it meant empty-headed. In James 2:20, it meant vain.

God will not be in hell. There will be no light in hell. It is the outer and utter darkness.

> Matthew 8:12 "But the sons of the kingdom be cast out into outer darkness. There will be weeping and gnashing of teeth." (See also Matthew 22:13.)

The sons of the kingdom, Jews who have not accepted Jesus as their Savior, will be cast into hell. Here in this eternal darkness, they, His people who died without the covering (wedding garment) of the righteousness blood of Jesus (Matthew. 22:11–13), will be cut off from the presence of God forever.

Jude's warning is about getting right with God by aligning your earthly relationships with the commands of God because you do not know when judgment day will come. ~~The Lord will deliver the godly out of temptations and reserve punishment for the un~~just.

> 2 Peter 2:6–10 "and turning the cities of Sodom and Gomorrah into ashes, condemned them to destruction, making them an example to those who afterward would live ungodly; [7]and delivered righteous Lot, who was oppressed by the filthy conduct of the wicked [8](for that righteous man, dwelling among them, tormented his righteous soul from day to day by seeing and hearing their lawless deeds)—[9]then the Lord know how to deliver the godly out of temptations and to reserve the unjust under punishment for the day of judgment [10]and especially those who walk according to the flesh in the lust of uncleanness and despise authority."

Many reject the thought of the eternal, unquenchable fire, which Scripture describes as just one of the attributes of hell, even though it is evidenced in Scripture.

> Matthew 18:8 "If your hand or foot causes you to sin, cut it off and cast it from you. It is better for you to enter into life lame or maimed, rather than having two hands or two feet, to be cast into the everlasting fire."

Matthew 25:41 "Then He will also say to those on the left hand, depart from Me, you cursed, into the everlasting fire prepared for the devil and his angels."

Life Application Questions

- What does it mean when Jude says "in a similar manner" in regards to the cities around Sodom and Gomorrah?
- Do you see any correlations between Sodom and Gomorrah and America today?
- Do you believe that hell is real?
- Do you believe that God will execute the vengeance of eternal fire on judgment day for those who have not repented of their sins, including their walk in the lusts of the flesh?

Verse 8

"Likewise also these dreamers defile the flesh, reject authority, and speak evil of dignitaries."

Likewise also these dreamers

Jude continues in his description of the wicked who "have crept in unnoticed" (verse 4) among the fellowship of believers. A "dreamer" chooses to dream up his own reality rather than live in God's reality and would follow the desires of his own flesh rather than bring every thought captive to the obedience of Christ. A dreamer can also dream up his own concepts of God under a covering of false religion or false prophecies.

These wicked men, "dreamers," are the ones spoken of in the Apostle Paul's exhortation in 2 Corinthians on spiritual warfare. In 2 Corinthians 10:5, he provides instruction for bringing these dreamers into obedience.

> 2 Corinthians 10:5 "Casting down arguments and every high thing that exalts itself against the knowledge of God, bringing every thought into captivity to the obedience of Christ."

The King James Version puts it, "Casting down imaginations . . ." The New American Standard Bible says, "We are destroying speculations and every lofty thing raised up against the knowledge of God, and we are taking every thought captive to the obedience of Christ."

These "dreams" are "imaginations," "speculations," or "arguments" need to be "cast down," not picked up by the faithful believers. The three characteristics mentioned by Jude—defile the flesh, reject authority, and speak evil of dignitaries—would be natural results of being a "dreamer."

Defile the flesh

To defile means to corrupt, pollute, contaminate, or stain. Since a "dreamer" replaces God's truth with his own fleshy imaginations, he would naturally "defile the flesh" by sinful living. A powerful illustration of this is found in the Bible.

> Romans 1:18–32 "For the wrath of God is revealed from heaven against all ungodliness and unrighteousness of men, who suppress the truth in unrighteousness, [19]because what may be known of God is manifest in them, for God has shown it to them. [20]For since the creation of the world His invisible attributes are clearly seen, being understood by the things that are made, even His eternal power and Godhead, so that they are without excuse, [21]because, although they knew God, they did not glorify Him as God, nor were thankful, but became futile in their thoughts, and their foolish hearts were darkened. [22]Professing to be wise, they became fools, [23]and changed the glory of the incorruptible God into an image made like corruptible man—and birds and four-footed animals and creeping things. [24]Therefore God also gave them up to uncleanness, in the lusts of their hearts, to dishonor their bodies among themselves, [25]who exchanged the truth of God for the lie, and worshiped and served the creature rather than the Creator, who is blessed forever. Amen. [26]For this reason God gave them up to vile passions. For even their women exchanged the natural use for what is against nature. [27]Likewise also the men, leaving the natural use of the woman, burned in their lust for one another, men with men committing what is shameful, and receiving in

themselves the penalty of their error which was due. [28]And even as they did not like to retain God in their knowledge, God gave them over to a debased mind, to do those things which are not fitting; [29]being filled with all unrighteousness, sexual immorality, wickedness, covetousness, maliciousness; full of envy, murder, strife, deceit, evil-mindedness; they are whisperers, [30]backbiters, haters of God, violent, proud, boasters, inventors of evil things, disobedient to parents, [31]undiscerning, untrustworthy, unloving, unforgiving, unmerciful; [32]who, knowing the righteous judgment of God, that those who practice such things are deserving of death, not only do the same but also approve of those who practice them."

God's judgment is a fact. Rejection of the knowledge of God (unbelief), as previously noted when Jude speaks of the Israelites, will bring the judgment of God upon a person. Unbelief brings tragic results.

Another example of judgment can be found in the book of I Corinthians.

1 Corinthians 3:17 "If anyone defiles the temple of God. God will destroy him. For the temple of God is holy, which *temple* you are."

The human body is God's temple.

1 Corinthians 6:19–20 "Or do you not know that your body is the temple of the Holy Spirit who is in you, who you have from God, and you are not your own? [20]For you were bought at a price; therefore glorify God in your body and in your spirit, which are God's."

You are God's precious child "bought with a price (I Corinthians 16:20)". Your freedom to choose His way for your life is secured in the love of God for you, His "precious child." Do not despair and do not lose heart.

God has spoken in His word, "believe" on the Lord Jesus Christ and you will be "saved" (Acts 16:31, Mark 16:16, John 3:16). God will even help you to exercise your power to choose.

You just have to ask, "Ask and it shall be given unto you (Matthew 7:7, Luke 11:9)." God's desire is that His children should not perish but that all would believe, repent and dwell with Him forever (2 Peter 3:9).

Reject authority

This means to refuse to accept leaders and/or that which is a source of right direction. A dreamer, as spoken of here, loves to live in his own dreamt-up world, and his own imagination governs him. He would naturally reject God's authority and commands regarding those in authority over man.

The rebellious children of Israel are a good example of what happens when we reject authority. They rejected both the authority of Moses and Aaron and the authority of God's commands that were being taught. God was not pleased.

> Numbers 16:3, 12–13 "They gathered together against Moses and Aaron, and said to them, 'you take too much upon yourselves, for all the congregation is holy, every one of them, and the LORD is among them. Why then do you exalt yourselves above the assembly of the LORD?' [12]And Moses sent to call Dathan and Abiram the sons of Eliab, but they said, "We will not come up! [13]Is it a small thing that you have brought us up out of a land flowing with milk and honey, to kill us in the wilderness, that you should keep acting like a prince over us?"

And when they realized that God was going to bring judgment upon them, they repented, that is, fell on their faces.

> Numbers 16:44 "And the LORD spoke to Moses, saying ⁴⁵Get away from among this congregation, that I may consume them in a moment. And they fell on their faces."

False teachers and dreamers reject the authority of God's commands. God's commandments call for us to respect, honor, and submit to those in authority when they do not cause us to violate the commands of God. God will hold those in authority accountable, so it is profitable for us to obey rather than reject.

> Romans 13:1–2 "Let every soul be subject to the governing authorities. For there is no authority except from God, and the authorities that exist are appointed by God. ²Therefore whoever resists the authority resists the ordinance of God, and those who resist will bring judgment on themselves."

> Hebrews 13:17 "Obey those who rule over you, and be submissive, for they watch out for your souls, as those who must give account. Let them do so with joy and not with grief, for that would be unprofitable for you."

Speak evil of dignitaries

This means voicing wickedness upon someone of high official position or rank. Jude may be speaking of angelic authorities, whom God had sent to turn the people away from the false teachers. But the people despised and spoke ill about anyone who sought to bring them into a right relationship with God.

Second Peter 2:10–11 is a parallel passage to this passage in Jude. In this passage, the term "apostles" seem to refer to church leaders. This could have even been the apostles, whom even angles would not speak against.

> 2 Peter 2:10–12 "And especially those who walk according to the flesh in the lust of uncleanness and despise authority. They are presumptuous, self-willed. They are not afraid to speak evil of dignitaries, [11]whereas angels, who are greater in power and might, do not bring a reviling accusation against them before the LORD. [12]But these, like natural brute beasts made to be caught and destroyed, speak evil of the things they do not understand, and will utterly perish in their own corruption."

Life Application Questions

- What do the words "defile the flesh" mean to you in the context of your life?
- What does the words used in this verse, "reject authority," mean to you as it applies to your life?
- Do you hear people "speaking evil of dignitaries" in today's world?
- How does it affect you?

VERSE 9

"Yet Michael the archangel, in contending with the devil, when he disputed about the body of Moses, dared not bring against him a reviling accusation, but said, "The LORD rebuke you!""

Yet Michael the archangel

An archangel is one of the highest ranking of God's angels. Michael is mentioned several times throughout the Scriptures, and he seems to be a powerful angel of war.

> Revelation 12:7–8 "And war broke out in heaven: Michael and his angels fought with the dragon; and the dragon and his angels fought, [8]but they did not prevail, nor was a place found for them in heaven any longer."

Michael is also called a "prince" in the book of Daniel.

> Daniel 10:13 "Michael, one of the chief princes, came to help me . . ."

> Daniel 12:1 "At that time Michael shall stand up, the great prince who stands watch over the sons of your people;"

In contending with the Devil, when he disputed about the body of Moses, dared not bring against him a reviling accusation, but said, "the LORD rebuke you!"

We do not have a record in Scripture of this event, but Bible scholars hypothesize that Jude could be quoting from a well-known extra-biblical writing of his time. Among the possibilities are the Book of Enoch, the Testament of Moses, and/or the Assumption of Moses.

The dispute is noted to be that the Devil claims he had a right to the body of Moses because of the murder Moses committed against the Egyptian spoken of in Exodus 2:12. Moses, like us, was certainly prone to having moments of disobedience to God. But he was God's man, who walked and talked in a personal relationship with God.

> Exodus 40:16 "Thus Moses did: according to all that the LORD had commanded him, so he did."

You can read of the death of Moses in Deuteronomy 34. We do know that the Devil did not gain possession of the body of Moses (as some have claimed) because Moses later appeared in bodily form at Jesus's transfiguration.

> Matthew 17:3 "And behold, Moses and Elijah appeared to them, talking with Him (Jesus)."

Jude is showing us that no one except God, not even a high-ranking angel like Michael, has authority to accuse or judge and/or pronounce punishment.

> Psalm 75:7 "But God is the Judge: He puts down one, And exalts another."

> James 4:12 "There is one Lawgiver, who is able to save and to destroy. Who are you to judge another?"

Bring against him a reviling accusation

This means to make a reproaching charge, with or without punishment. Michael knew better than to speak against the Devil, who possibly at one time ranked higher than Michael. Michael did take a stand, contend, against the Devil for the body of Moses, but he did not stand in his own authority. His stand was in the authority of the LORD. He said, "The LORD rebuke you!" standing only in the authority and in the name of the LORD. We should follow his example.

Another example of this is found in Zechariah.

> Zechariah 3:1–2. "Then he showed me Joshua the high priest standing before the Angel of the LORD, and Satan standing at his right hand to oppose him. ²And the LORD said to Satan, 'The LORD rebuke you, Satan! The LORD who has chosen Jerusalem rebuke you! Is this not a brand plucked from the fire?'"

The great archangel Michael and Joshua, God's chosen leader of the Israelites, were careful how they addressed the Devil, who once was a great "dignitary" of God but now stood in opposition to God's authority. They set an example for us in dealing with those in opposition to God's authority.

"The LORD rebuke you." The word "rebuke" is also translated to reprove or charged, which also means convict in some translations. There are several examples of Jesus, God's son, rebuking unclean spirits.

> Matthew 17:18 "And Jesus rebuked the demon, and it came out of him; and the child was cured from that very hour."

> Mark 1:25 "But Jesus rebuked him, saying, 'Be quiet, and come out of him!'"

Mark 9:25 "When Jesus saw that the people came running together, He rebuked the unclean spirit, saying to it, 'Deaf and dumb spirit, I command you, come out of him and enter him no more!'"

Luke 4:35, 41 "But Jesus rebuked him, saying, "Be quiet, and come out of him!" And when the demon had thrown him in their midst, it came out of him and did not hurt him. [41]And demons also came out of many, crying out and saying, "You are the Christ, the Son of God!" And He, rebuking them, did not allow them to speak, for they knew that He was the Christ."

Luke 9:42–43 "And as he was still coming, the demon threw him down and convulsed him. Then Jesus rebuked the unclean spirit, healed the child, and gave him back to his father. [43]And they were all amazed at the majesty of God. But while everyone marveled at all the things which Jesus did, He said to His disciples,"

Life Application Questions

- How did Michael the archangel handle his encounter with Satan?
- How can this lesson be applied to your life?
- Do you believe that God and God alone has the power to judge and defeat Satan and the forces of evil?
- How does this affect the way you live?

Verse 10

"But these speak evil of whatever they do not know; and whatever they know naturally, like brute beasts, in these things they corrupt themselves."

But these speak evil of whatever they do not know

"These" dreamers and false prophets are people saying destructive things about subjects and knowledge that they don't even know anything about. They are pretending or dreaming, or they are deceivers with plans to bring others into corruption with their words. Their speech may have included gossip, slander, and/or judgment.

This example is placed here to show the vast difference between Michael, who shows proper respect, and those who scorn God's authority. This comparison shows the stark contrast between those in submission to God and His dignitaries and those who dream of their own rule and authority.

Jude gives us an example in Michael, who sets an example for us in showing proper respect for boundaries and God's authority in dealing with those in opposition to God's authority.

And whatever they know naturally, like brute beasts, in these things they corrupt themselves

These dreamers and false prophets are living out their own teaching. Like brute beasts of the field, who instinctively follow their own desire and passions, these false teachers and dreamers have become slaves to their own passions and will corrupt themselves.

Jude issues this warning that this kind of behavior brings corruption. Like brute beasts, those who reject God's authority have become cunning, natural predators of those who are weak, unhealthy, and vulnerable, making them dangerous to those around them.

God speaks of beasts as one of the four forms of destruction God would bring upon His people when He became so angry with them for what Manasseh, king of Judah, did in Jerusalem that He would not even accept the intercession of Moses or Samuel.

> Jeremiah 15:3 "'And I will appoint over them four forms of destruction,' says the LORD: 'the sword to slay, the dogs to drag the birds of the heavens and the beast of the earth to devour and destroy.'"

Peter says these brute (wild) beasts are made to be caught in God's judgment because "gut instincts" dominate them and they lack true understanding.

> 2 Peter 2:12 "But these, like natural brute beasts made to be caught and destroyed, speak evil of the things they do not understand, and will utterly perish in their own corruption."

The spiritual digression that comes from unbelief and foolish and darkened hearts is spoken of in Romans.

> Romans 1:21–28 "Because, although they knew God, they did not glorify Him as God, nor were thankful, but became futile in their thoughts, and their foolish hearts were darkened. ²²Professing to be wise, they became fools, ²³and changed the glory of the incorruptible God into an image made like corruptible man—and birds and four-footed animals and creeping things. ²⁴Therefore God also gave them up to uncleanness, in the lusts of their hearts, to dishonor their

bodies among themselves, [25]who exchanged the truth of God for the lie, and worshiped and served the creature rather than the Creator, who is blessed forever. Amen. [26]For this reason God gave them up to vile passions. For even their women exchanged the natural use for what is against nature. [27]Likewise also the men, leaving the natural use of the woman, burned in their lust for one another, men with men committing what is shameful, and receiving in themselves the penalty of their error which was due. [28]And even as they did not like to retain God in their knowledge, God gave them over to a debased mind, to do those things which are not fitting."

But God wants all to be saved.

1 Timothy 2:4 "Who desires all men to be saved and to come to the knowledge of the truth."

2 Peter 3:9 "The LORD is not slack concerning His promise, as some count slackness, but is longsuffering toward us, not willing that any should perish but that all should come to repentance."

And He will continually pursue you.

Psalm 23:6 "Surely goodness and mercy shall follow me all the days of my life; and I will dwell in the house of the LORD forever."

Those who are evil may even be turned over to Satan so they might be saved.

1 Corinthians 5:5 "Deliver such a one to Satan for the destruction of the flesh, that his spirit may be saved in the day of the LORD Jesus."

But what Satan means for evil, God will use for good.

> Genesis 50:20 "But as for you, you meant evil against me; but God meant it for good, in order to bring it about as it is this day, to save many people alive."

Christians being sent out amongst the wolves, those who speak and act in an evil manner, are to follow God's warning and instruction in Matthew.

> Matthew 10:16–19 (Jesus speaking) "Behold, I send you out as sheep in the midst of wolves. Therefore be wise as serpents and harmless as doves. [17]But beware of men, for they will deliver you up to councils and scourge you in their synagogues. [18]You will be brought before governors and kings for My sake, as a testimony to them and to the Gentiles. [19]But when they deliver you up, do not worry about how or what you should speak. For it will be given to you in that hour what you should speak; [20]for it is not you who speak, but the Spirit of your Father who speaks in you."

Life Application Questions

- What do the words "speak evil of what they do not know" mean to you?
- How can this be applied to your life?
- How does one become a slave to evil even when he has been shown God's way?
- What are God's children to do when faced with the wolves/evil of the world?

Verse 11

"Woe to them! For they have gone in the way of Cain, have run greedily in the error of Balaam for profit, and perished in the rebellion of Korah."

Woe to them!

A "woe" is a despair and misery. Jude is speaking of the false teachers, dreamers, and the ungodly who are mentioned previously. There are Old Testament references to woe. Jesus often declared a woe on religious hypocrites and those deserving God's judgment.

> Isaiah 3:9 "The look on their countenance witnesses against them, and they declare their sin as Sodom; Woe to their soul! For they have brought evil upon themselves."

> Isaiah 3:11 "Woe to the wicked! It shall be ill with him."

> Ezekiel 13:3 "Thus says the LORD: 'Woe to the foolish prophets, who follow their own sprit and have seen nothing."

> Matthew 23:14 "Woe to blind guides, who say, 'whoever swears by the temple, it is nothing: but whomever swear by gold of the temple, he is obliged to perform it'."

> Luke 11:46 "And He said 'woe to you also, lawyers! For you
> load men with burdens to bear, and you yourselves do not
> touch the burdens with one of your fingers.'"

Jude gives us three examples of men gone bad: the way of Cain, the error of Baalam, and the rebellion of Korah.

For they have gone in the way of Cain

Cain was the son of Adam and Eve and the brother of Abel. You can read of his story in Genesis 4. Cain and his brother both made an offering to the LORD. God accepted Abel's offering and rejected Cain's. This made Cain jealous and angry. Cain let these fleshly feelings take over, and he murdered his own brother. New Testament writers give more insight to this event.

> Hebrews 11:4 "By faith Abel offered to God a more excellent
> sacrifice than Cain, though which he obtained witness that
> he was righteous, God testifying of his gifts; and through it
> he being dead still speaks."

> 1 John 3:12 "Not as Cain who was the wicked one and
> murdered his brother. And why did he murder him? Because
> his works were evil and his brother's righteous."

The way of Cain was the way of self-serving, youthful lusts, unbelief, and unrighteousness distinguished by jealousy, hatred, and murder. Cain wanted to do things his way and have God accept it; Abel wanted to please God.

Have run greedily in the error of Balaam for profit

Balaam was a prophet of God. Balaam would obey and serve God and then, in error, turn right around and go his own way. Balaam's error may have been a bitterroot judgment (Hebrews 12:14, James 3:13–18) that brought forth the fruit of greed and therefore defiled him.

You can read his story in Numbers 22–25 and 31. King Balak of the Moabites hired the prophet Balaam to curse Israel because he knew he could not defeat them by natural means. Every time Balaam tried to curse Israel, he ended up pronouncing a blessing upon them instead of a curse.

God would not let Balaam curse His people. Yet because Balaam greatly desired the financial or material rewards that King Balak offered him, he finally gave the king advice that would bring destruction upon God's people. Balaam counseled King Balak that sexual and spiritual idolatry could bring down the children of Israel. King Balak sent the women of Moab to seduce the young Israeli soldiers and then entice them to worship their gods.

> Numbers 31:16 "Look these women caused the children of Israel, through the counsel of Balaam, to trespass against the LORD in incident of Peor, and there was a plague among the congregation of the LORD."

This man-plan brought great destruction upon the people of God. Balaam's greedy error was to think he could use his God-given position to profit himself rather than for God's glory.

After giving a discourse to Balak regarding God's faithfulness, Balaam told Balak that he must do what God told him to do. His mouth spoke, but his heart was never changed, or a bitterroot defiled or weakened him. Balaam continued to carry out God's instruction from a self-serving attitude rather than fully seeking first the kingdom of God and surrendering to the fullness of righteousness living, God's way.

> Numbers 23:26 "But Balaam answered and said to Balak, 'Did I not tell you, saying, All the LORD speaks, that I must do?'"

Balaam wavered, and he was unstable. He couldn't be trusted to follow God every step of the way. The greed that defiled him led to Balaam's own destruction. In God's providence, the very people against whom he had given his wicked counsel slew Balaam.

> Numbers 31:8 "They killed the kings of Midian with the rest of those who were killed—Evi, Rekem, Zur, Hur, and Reba, the five kings of Midian. Balaam the son of Beor they also killed with the sword."

And perished in the rebellion of Korah

Korah was caught in his own rebellious state and took those whom he misled into destruction with him. Korah is the third example given by Jude of how a person numbered among God's people, even among God's leaders, can turn to folly and destruction.

You can read about Korah and his rebellion in Numbers 16. Korah, a Levite and prominent leader in Israel, had been given the high honor of overseeing the transport of the holy items of the tabernacle. Korah was not satisfied with the position of honor God had given him. He even challenged Moses's authority. When the contest was over, all who sided with Korah were destroyed as the ground opened up and swallowed them. The sin of pride and rebellion brought destruction.

Korah's story demonstrates a truth. When you rebel against the people God has raised up in authority, you rebel against the LORD Himself.

> Numbers 16:32 "And the earth opened its mouth and swallowed them up, with their households and all the men with Korah, with all their goods."

Korah perished.

The three examples given above are powerful illustrations of how people from various backgrounds and status can start out or appear to be in good standing with God and end up in opposition to God. The result is always disastrous.

Life Application Questions

- What does the "way of Cain" mean? How does this apply to your life?
- What does the "error of Balaam" mean? How does this apply to your life?
- What does the "rebellion of Korah" mean? How does this apply to your life?

Verse 12

"These are spots in your love feasts, while they feast with you without fear, serving only themselves. They are clouds without water, carried about by the winds; late autumn trees without fruit, twice dead, pulled up by the roots;"

These are spots in your love feasts

The early Christians had a practice of meeting together regularly for a time of food and fellowship. Today, we might call these meetings "potlucks" or "food faiths." The early Christians called these meetings "love feasts."

Jude is speaking of the apostates who "have crept in unnoticed" (verse 4), and without fear, they are causing spots in their love feasts. This describes a scene in which all is beautiful in a gathering of Christian love and sharing except for these ugly spots. Some commentaries also call these spots "rocks that are hard to get over." These spots or rocks taint or spoil the beauty of Christian fellowship and relationships with both God and man.

An apostate has abandoned his or her religion and principles. An apostate commits apostasies, those things that show/demonstrate that one has turned from God.

Compare Jude 12 with 2 Peter 2:13–14.

> 2 Peter 13–14 "And will receive the wages of unrighteousness, as those who count it pleasure to carouse in the daytime. They are spots and blemishes, carousing in their own deceptions while they feast with you, ¹⁴having eyes full of

adultery and that cannot cease from sin, enticing unstable souls. They have a heart trained in covetous practices, and are accursed children."

While they feast with you without fear

The apostates come in and feast (eat), not being afraid of being discovered or ashamed. These false Christians, whom Jude has already described as "ungodly" (verse 4), "brute beasts" (verse 10), and "dreamers" (verse 8), continue to mingle with the faithful with no fear of God or people. They act as if nothing is wrong and continue to serve themselves only. Their actions deceive both themselves and others.

Serving only themselves

The apostates are the ungodly, brute beasts, dreamers, and false teachers who seek only their self-satisfaction and therefore serve only themselves. They have turned from the way God planned.

In the previous verse, Jude gave the examples of those who served only themselves. Cain, Baalam, and Korah are examples of lives lived in the opposition to God's plan for the Christian life and standard, which is to be a servant of God and a servant of others.

> Mark 10:42–45 "But Jesus called them to Himself and said to them, "You know that those who are considered rulers over the Gentiles LORD it over them, and their great ones exercise authority over them. 43Yet it shall not be so among you; but whoever desires to become great among you shall be your servant. 44And whoever of you desires to be first shall be slave of all. 45For even the Son of Man did not come to be served, but to serve, and to give His life a ransom for many."

Christians are to die to self and live unto God

Mark 8:34 "Who ever desires to come after Me, let him deny himself and take up his cross, and follow Me."

Romans 6:11 "likewise you also, reckon yourself to be dead indeed to sin, but alive to God in Christ Jesus our LORD."

These "certain men" (verse 4) live by a "self-serving" philosophy.

They are clouds without water

A cloud without water is not a real cloud because it does not fulfill God's purpose for clouds. It brings no blessing of rain to water the earth. Likewise, these men Jude is describing are not real Christians. The refreshing spiritual blessing that God intended Christians to bring to others is not there.

Carried about by the winds

The various winds of doctrine that come from the spirit of error blow or carry about these "spots." The winds of doctrine are an unseen man or evil-driven force, gentle or strong, that directs or changes teaching and the body of values and principles from which the teaching within the church is derived. The Scriptures give clear warning about being carried about by every wind of doctrine.

Ephesians 4:14 "That we should no longer be children, tossed to and fro and carried about with every wind of doctrine, by the trickery of men, in cunning craftiness of deceitful plotting."

James 1:6 "But let him ask in faith, with no doubting, for he who doubts is like a wave of the sea driven and tossed by the wind."

The person who builds the foundation of his or her house of faith upon the rock of Jesus can stand against the winds. It is the foolish man who cannot.

> Matthew 7:24–27 (Jesus speaking) "Therefore whoever hears these sayings of Mine, and does them, I will liken him to a wise man who built his house on the rock: ²⁵and the rain descended, the floods came, and the winds blew and beat on that house; and it did not fall, for it was founded on the rock. ²⁶But everyone who hears these sayings of Mine, and does not do them, will be like a foolish man who built his house on the sand: ²⁷and the rain descended, the floods came, and the winds blew and beat on that house; and it fell. And great was its fall."

We can stand steadfast in our faith.

> Colossians 2:5 "For though I am absent in the flesh, yet I am with you in spirit, rejoicing to see your good order and the steadfastness of your faith in Christ."

Those persons who allow the work of the Holy Spirit in their lives are like eagles. They put themselves in position (mount up) upon a rock at a cliff's edge, and they are strong enough to extend their wings. They stand waiting for the winds with wings outspread. The winds come up under their wings and lift them to soar to their destination.

> Isaiah 40:31 "But those who wait upon the LORD shall renew their strength; They shall mount up with wings like eagles, They shall run and not be weary, They shall walk and not faint."

And when the storm rages and the winds blow, we are to put down anchor and pray, just as Paul did in the storm on the voyage to Rome.

Acts 27:29 "Then, fearing lest we should run aground on the rocks, they dropped four anchors from the stern, and prayed for day to come."

Some examples of people following "winds of doctrine" are in the New Testament. The Galatians were being carried about and turning away to a "wind of doctrine," presented by a heretical group (Galatians 1:6). Their counterfeit (called "bewitching" in 3:1) gospel combined salvation through Christ with adherence to the procedures of the Mosaic Law in Judaism. Paul warned them that choosing to obtain salvation by the law was denying the necessity of Jesus's death on the cross.

Galatians 1:6–10 "I marvel that you are turning away so soon from Him who called you in the grace of Christ, to a different gospel, [7]which is not another; but there are some who trouble you and want to pervert the gospel of Christ. [8]But even if we, or an angel from heaven, preach any other gospel to you than what we have preached to you, let him be accursed. [9]As we have said before, so now I say again, if anyone preaches any other gospel to you than what you have received, let him be accursed. [10]For do I now persuade men, or God? Or do I seek to please men? For if I still pleased men, I would not be a bondservant of Christ."

The Colossians were being carried about and accepting "winds of doctrine" that were similar to the Galatians. Paul writes to them to expose the truth. They are subjecting themselves to regulations that only have the appearance of wisdom but are of no value against the lusts of the flesh.

Colossians 2:20–23 "Therefore, if you died with Christ from the basic principles of the world, why, as though living in the world, do you subject yourselves to regulations (see also 1 Timothy 4:3)—[21]'Do not touch, do not taste, do not handle,' [22]which all concern things which perish with the using—according to the commandments and doctrines of men? (See also Isaiah 29:13 and Matthew 15:9.) [23]These things indeed have an appearance of wisdom in self-imposed religion, false humility, and neglect of the body, but are of no value against the indulgence of the flesh."

For additional study, see references from the preceding Scripture.

1 Timothy 4:3 "Forbidding to marry, and commanding to abstain from foods which God created to be received with thanksgiving by those who believe and know the truth."

Isaiah 29:13 "Therefore the LORD said: "Inasmuch as these people draw near with their mouths and honor Me with their lips, but have removed their hearts far from Me, and their fear toward Me is taught by the commandment of men"

Matthew 15:9 (Jesus speaking) "And in vain they worship Me, teaching as doctrines the commandments of men."

The Acts of the Apostles, namely miracles, stirred the people, and they began to reason falsely (form a "wind of doctrine" from their own minds). They began to worship created beings in the form of the disciples, believing them to be the false gods, Zeus and Hermes, rather than worshipping the Creator.

Acts 14:8–21 "And in Lystra a certain man without strength in his feet was sitting, a cripple from his mother's womb, who had never walked. [9]This man heard Paul speaking. Paul, observing him intently and seeing that he had faith to be healed, [10]said with a loud voice, "Stand up straight on your feet!" And he leaped and walked. [11]Now when the people saw what Paul had done, they raised their voices, saying in the Lycaonian language, "The gods have come down to us in the likeness of men!" [12]And Barnabas they called Zeus, and Paul, Hermes, because he was the chief speaker. [13]Then the priest of Zeus, whose temple was in front of their city, brought oxen and garlands to the gates, intending to sacrifice with the multitudes."

When Paul and Barnabas realized this "wind of doctrine" was carrying them about, they tore their clothes and began teaching (declaring the Truth).

Acts 14:14 "But when the apostles Barnabas and Paul heard this, they tore their clothes and ran in among the multitude, crying out [15]and saying, "Men, why are you doing these things? We also are men with the same nature as you, and preach to you that you should turn from these useless things to the living God, who made the heaven, the earth, the sea, and all things that are in them, [16]who in bygone generations allowed all nations to walk in their own ways. [17]Nevertheless He did not leave Himself without witness, in that He did good, gave us rain from heaven and fruitful seasons, filling our hearts with food and gladness." [18]And with these sayings they could scarcely restrain the multitudes from sacrificing to them."

God restrained the "wind of doctrine" that had come from man's mind and strengthened the disciples, and they carried on so the door of faith was opened to the Gentiles.

Acts 14:19 "Then Jews from Antioch and Iconium came there; and having persuaded the multitudes, they stoned Paul and dragged him out of the city, supposing him to be dead. [20]However, when the disciples gathered around

him, he rose up and went into the city. And the next day
he departed with Barnabas to Derbe. ²¹And when they had
preached the gospel to that city and made many disciples,
they returned to Lystra, Iconium, and Antioch,"

Certain men taught a "wind of doctrine" in reference to
circumcision.

Acts 15:1–2 "And certain men came down from Judea and
taught the brethren, "Unless you are circumcised according
to the custom of Moses, you cannot be saved." ²Therefore,
when Paul and Barnabas had no small dissension and
dispute with them, they determined that Paul and Barnabas
and certain others of them should go up to Jerusalem, to the
apostles and elders, about this question."

The matter became serious enough. The wind of doctrine was
carrying many people about, and confusion was resulting. So a
conference was called in Jerusalem. They brought together men of God
to seek God in this matter.

Acts 15:6 "Now the apostles and elders came together to
consider this matter."

The Jerusalem Decision was that circumcision was not necessary.
But it was decided that all would abstain from things offered to idols,
from blood and from strangled things, so both Jews and Christians
could remain in fellowship. Sexual immorality was forbidden for
everyone. (This received emphasis because it was a prominent sin
among the Gentiles.)

Acts 15:24–29 "Since we have heard that some who went out
from us have troubled you with words, unsettling your souls,
saying, "You must be circumcised and keep the law"—to

whom we gave no such commandment—[25]it seemed good to us, being assembled with one accord, to send chosen men to you with our beloved Barnabas and Paul, [26]men who have risked their lives for the name of our LORD Jesus Christ. [27]We have therefore sent Judas and Silas, who will also report the same things by word of mouth. [28]For it seemed good to the Holy Spirit, and to us, to lay upon you no greater burden than these necessary things: [29]that you abstain from things offered to idols, from blood, from things strangled, and from sexual immorality. If you keep yourselves from these, you will do well. Farewell."

They were asked to abstain from things offered to idols, from blood and from things strangled, so they were able to be all things to the Jews, whom they sought to bring into the Light. Also see Jude verse 4 notes on lewdness for another example.

Late autumn trees without fruit

By late autumn, mature, healthy trees should have produced fruit. Jude uses a word, "picture," to illustrate that these men or women, who are supposed to be mature, late autumn trees, are not living in true Christian character and are not bearing the fruit that is expected of one in his or her later years. True Christians bear fruit.

In John 15:1–9 "Christ tells the parable about the vine dresser and how He prunes the vines so that it will bear fruit and how He removes the non fruit bearing branches."

Galatians 5:22–24 "But the fruit of the Spirit is love, joy, peace, longsuffering, kindness, goodness, faithfulness, [23]gentleness, self-control. Against such there is no law. [24]And those who are Christ's have crucified the flesh with its passions and desires."

Ephesians 5:8–11 "For you were once darkness, but now
you are light in the LORD. Walk as children of light ⁹(for
the fruit of the Spirit is in all goodness, righteousness, and
truth), ¹⁰finding out what is acceptable to the LORD ¹¹And
have no fellowship with the unfruitful works of darkness,
but rather expose them."

These men and women are takers. They are not being the givers
God intended them to be. They are like trees without fruit. They
occupy ground and use up resources but never give anything back in
return.

We are to have no fellowship with the unfruitful works of darkness,
but we are to expose them (Ephesians 5:11). We have been told that
this includes the works of false prophets, dreamers, and apostates. We
have also been told that God will bring judgment. But how can we
recognize them so we can obey God's instructions?

Matthew 7:15–16 (Jesus speaking) "Beware of false prophets,
who come to you in sheep's clothing, but inwardly they are
ravenous wolves. ¹⁶You will know them by their fruits. Do
men gather grapes from thornbushes or figs from thistles?"

You will recognize them (late autumn trees) by examining their fruit.
By their fruit, you will know whether or not they are a true follower of
Christ. But we are to be like the certain man in Jesus' parable of the fig
tree and be willing to cultivate these trees so they might produce.

Luke 13:6–9 "He (Jesus) also spoke this parable: "A certain
man had a fig tree planted in his vineyard, and he came
seeking fruit on it and found none. ⁷Then he said to the
keeper of his vineyard, 'Look, for three years I have come
seeking fruit on this fig tree and find none. Cut it down;
why does it use up the ground?' ⁸But he answered and said
to him, 'Sir, let it alone this year also, until I dig around it

and fertilize it. ⁹And if it bears fruit, well. But if not, after that you can cut it down.'"

Twice dead

This is another way to describe an apostate. They were once dead in their own sin, but God had made them alive when they first believed, but they have died again in their own sin and refusal to believe.

> Ephesians 2:1 "and you He made alive, who were dead in trespasses and sins."

> Ephesians 2:5 "even when we were dead in trespasses, made us alive together with Christ (by grace you have been saved)."

> Colossians 2:13 "and you being dead in your trespasses, and the uncircumcision of your flesh, He has made alive together with Him, having forgiven you all trespasses,"

Then, after receiving the life given to them by God, they became dead again by turning from the true faith.

> Hebrews 6:4–8 "For it is impossible for those who were once enlightened, and have tasted the heavenly gift, and have become partakers of the Holy Spirit, ⁵and have tasted the good word of God and the powers of the age to come, ⁶if they fall away, to renew them again to repentance, since they crucify again for themselves the Son of God, and put Him to an open shame. ⁷For the earth which drinks in the rain that often comes upon it, and bears herbs useful for those by whom it is cultivated, receives blessing from God; ⁸but if it bears thorns and briers, it is rejected and near to being cursed, whose end is to be burned."

They are twice dead.

Pulled up by the roots

A tree that bore no fruit and was pulled up by its roots would likewise become twice dead.

> John 15:6 (Jesus speaking) "If anyone does not abide in Me, he is cast out as a branch and is withered; and they gather them and throw them into the fire, and they are burned."

A tree with unstable roots loses its anchor hold. The wind is able to toss about a tree without a firm root system. The unstable root system may become unable to sustain the tree in a manner that allows the tree to remain in an upright position and fill its place in the environment. An unstable tree must be removed (pulled up by its roots) to maintain safe conditions around it.

Life Application Questions

- What does the Scripture tell us to use as a test to determine if a person is a true follower of Christ?
- How can a person be twice dead?
- How are God's children to handle the unfruitful works of darkness?
- What does the Bible say God will do with someone who does not bear fruit?

VERSE 13

"Raging waves of the sea, foaming up their own shame; wandering stars for whom is reserved the blackness of darkness forever."

Raging waves of the sea, foaming up their own shame

This is another word picture of the wicked, those who have either made or followed a path of darkness, self-serving, or false teaching, and they have set their minds on earthly things and commit deeds that are against God's law. These wicked ones will rage and bring up impurities in the same manner as sea foam.

> Isaiah 57:20–21 "But the wicked are like the troubled sea, when it cannot rest, whose waters cast up mire and dirt. [21]'There is no peace,' says my God, 'for the wicked.'"

The manner of impurities will be our own shame, disgrace, and dishonor.

> Romans 12:24–25 "Therefore God also gave them up to uncleanness, in the lusts of their hearts, to dishonor their bodies among themselves [25]who exchanged the truth of God for the lie, and worshiped and served the creature rather than the Creator, who is blessed forever, Amen."

God will restore the repentant, but His peace is not available to those who persist in their wickedness.

> Psalm 1:6 "For the LORD knows the way of the righteous,
> but the way of the ungodly shall perish."

The LORD knows and actively cares for the righteous, but the ungodly come to a dead end and will perish.

Wandering stars

The last word picture Jude uses to describe the apostates is a picture of a comet. A comet appears for a moment and flashes in the sky on its way to destruction, so these men show up on the scene for a moment and are then gone forever.

Navigation at sea or through life by charting your course using wandering stars would lead to disaster. Following these wandering stars (false teachers) is like charting your course at sea by a navigation instrument and techniques that are set on a fleeting changeable pattern rather than a stable pattern that functions with accuracy and regularity.

Even Christians are being deceived and accepting the words of these false teachers who teach that it is all right to indulge our lusts because Jesus has given us liberty from the law. The teachers themselves have been overcome by sin and have become slaves of moral corruption.

Peter also speaks about false teachers who promote immorality in 2 Peter 2:12–22. Verses 20–22 in particular have application in the study of this verse.

> 2 Peter 2:20–22 "For if, after they have escaped the pollutions of the world through the knowledge of the LORD and Savior Jesus Christ, they are again entangled in them and overcome, the latter end is worst for them than the beginning. [21]For it would have been better for them not to have known the way of righteousness, than having known it, to turn from the holy commandment delivered to them. [22]But it has happened to them according to the true proverb:

'a dog returns to his own vomit' and 'a sow having washed, to her wallowing in the mire.'"

For whom is reserved the blackness of darkness forever

This is a bleak picture of the outer "chains of darkness" reserved forever for those who reject God's salvation and rule.

Man was created to be an eternal being. He will spend eternity somewhere. There is no middle ground. Man will either spend eternity in heaven or hell—the blackness and loneliness of darkness and eternal fire and eternal unrest.

> Matthew 8:12 (Jesus speaking) "But the sons of the kingdom will be cast out into outer darkness. There will be weeping and gnashing of teeth."

> Matthew 22:13 (Jesus speaking) "Then the king said to the servant, 'bind him hand and foot, take him away, and cast him into outer darkness: there will be weeping and gnashing of teeth.'"

> Matthew 25:30 (Jesus speaking) "And cast the unprofitable servant into the outer darkness. There will be weeping and gnashing of teeth."

> 2 Peter 2:17 "These are wells without water, clouds carried by a tempest, for whom is reserved the blackness of darkness forever."

> Revelation 14:10–11 "He himself shall also drink of the wine of the wrath of God, which is poured out full strength into the cup of His indignation. He shall be tormented with fire and brimstone in the presence of the holy angels and in the presence of the Lamb. [11]And the smoke of their torment

ascends forever and ever; and they have no rest day or night, who worship the beast and his image, and whoever receives the mark of his name."

He himself is the Devil.

Revelation 20:10 "The devil, who deceived them, was cast into the lake of fire and brimstone where the beast and the false prophet are. And they will be tormented day and night forever and ever."

Revelation 21:8 "But the cowardly, unbelieving, abominable, murderers, sexually immoral, sorcerers, idolaters, ad all liars shall have their part in the lake which burns with fire and brimstone, which is the second death."

The cowardly are Christians who do not remain faithful under difficulties and persecution. Notice that those who forsake Christ are listed with those who commit the abominable sins.

Life Application Questions

- What picture do you get when you think of "raging waves of the sea foaming up their own shame"?
- What is an apostate?
- How would "wandering stars" affect navigation?
- How would following a false teacher affect your walk with God?
- Do you believe that, according to the Scriptures, we as humans are able to gain some understanding of the eternal consequences for living a life out of alignment with God's commands?

VERSE 14A

"Now Enoch, the seventh from Adam, prophesied about these men also, saying,"

Now Enoch, the seventh from Adam

Enoch was born the seventh generation after Adam (Genesis 5:3–23), the first man created by God. Seven is God's number of perfection. Enoch was the son of Jared and father of Methuselah. He was reported to have walked with God, and God took him. He did not face death, but God took him up into the heavenly realm because God was pleased with the faith of Enoch.

Enoch is presented as an example in the Old and New Testament as a man of faith. He was a man who pleased God so much that Enoch didn't have to face death. Enoch is a model for us to live by.

> Genesis 5:18, 24 "Jared lived one hundred and sixty-two years, and begot Enoch. 24And Enoch walked with God: and he was not, for God took him."

> Hebrews 11:5–6 "By faith Enoch was taken away so that he did not see death, and was not found, because God had taken him for before he was taken he had this testimony, that he pleased God. 6But without faith it is impossible to please Him, for he who comes to God must believe that He is, and that He is a rewarder of those who diligently seek Him."

Prophesied about these men, also saying

Enoch's prophecy warned about the coming judgment upon these men, false teachers and dreamers, but it was not included in the biblical canon of Scripture. However, God had Jude to write about this so we would know that Enoch, who walked and talked upon the Earth in ancient times as a mere mortal, pleased God with his faith. He was a prophet of God warning God's people of the dangers.

It is of interest that the book of Enoch's prophecies is said to have continued a prophecy of warning about the judgment that God would pronounce upon false teachers. This book was said to have been preserved by Noah in the ark. It was never accepted as authoritative Scripture. Yet Jews and the early Christians of Jude's day widely respected it.

Jude quotes extra-biblical writings several times in this short letter. (Compare verse 9.) Keep in mind that many great writings today are not held to the same level as Scripture, yet God can use them to bless us, His children.

God gives us instruction in His Word to help us to discern the truth from lies. Some extra-biblical writings are clearly fairy tales and do not align with the Bible. We are to test the words that we take to heart and choose to accept as guidelines for our life.

> 1 Thessalonians 5:21–22 "Test all things; hold fast what is good. 22Abstain from every form of evil."

> 1 Corinthians 14:29 "Let two or three prophets speak, and let the others judge."

> 1 John 4:1 "Beloved, do not believe every spirit, but test the spirits, whether they are of God; because many false prophets have gone out into the world."

The Truth is the author of peace and will not create confusion.

1 Corinthians 14:31–33 "For you can all prophesy one by one, that all may learn and all may be encouraged. [32]And the spirits of the prophets are subject to the prophets. [33]For God is not the author of confusion but of peace, as in all the churches of the saints."

Just as those who heard Paul's message in Berea tested the words of Paul, spoken of in Acts 17, we are to search for the truth in what we hear.

Acts 17:11 "These were more fair-minded than those in Thessalonica, in that they received the word with all readiness, and searched the Scriptures daily to find out whether these things were so."

Even though the only mention we have of Enoch's teaching on false teachers is in Jude, God has warned us sufficiently that those false teaching, vain words that go contrary to the law of God, is wrong and will be punished.

Exodus 23:7 "Keep yourself far from a false matter; do not kill the innocent and righteous. For I will not justify the wicked."

Proverbs 13:5 "a righteous man hates lying, But a wicked man is lathsome and comes to shame."

Exodus 5:9 "Let more work be laid on the men, that they may labor in it, and let them not regard false words."

Proverbs 6:12 "A worthless person, a wicked man, walks with a perverse mouth;"

Jeremiah 14:14 "And the LORD said to me, 'The prophets prophesy lies in My name. I have not sent them, commanded them, nor spoken to them; they prophesy to you a false vision, divination, a worthless thing, and the deceit of their heart.'"

Lamentations 2:14 "Your prophets have seen for you false and deceptive visions; they have not uncovered your iniquity, to bring back your captives, but have envisioned for you false prophecies and delusions."

Ezekiel 22:28 "Her prophets plastered them with untempered mortar, seeing false visions, and divining lies for them, saying, 'Thus says the LORD GOD,' when the LORD had not spoken."

Zechariah 10:2 "For the idols speak delusion; the diviners envision lies, and tell false dreams; they comfort in vain. Therefore the people wend their way like sheep; they are in trouble because there is no shepherd."

Mark 13:22 (Jesus speaking) "For false christs and false prophets will rise and show signs and wonders to deceive, if possible, even the elect."

2 Thessalonians 2:9 "The coming of the lawless one is according to the working of Satan, with all power, signs, and lying wonders,"

Revelation 2:2 (Jesus speaking) "I know your works, your labor, your patience, and that you cannot bear those who are evil. And you have tested those who say they are apostles and are not, and have found them liars;"

Life Application Questions

- How are we to handle Scripture that was never accepted as authoritative, for example, Enoch's prophecies?
- What does the Scripture say about handling new teachings?
- How can we, as God's children, live a life that is God-pleasing (like Enoch) and be an example of a man or woman of faith?

Verses 14b–15

"Behold, the LORD comes with ten thousands of His saints, ¹⁵to execute judgment on all, to convict all who are ungodly among them of all their ungodly deeds which they have committed in an ungodly way, and of all the harsh things which ungodly sinners have spoken against Him."

Behold

This means, "Attention. Something is to be seen"

The LORD comes

This means the LORD will arrive.

Ten thousand of His saints

Jesus will return someday with his saints to judge the world in righteousness

> Matthew 16:27: "For the Son of Man will come in the glory of His Father with His angels, and them He will reward each according to his works."

> 1 Corinthians 6:2 "Do you know that the saints will judge the world?"

Ungodly

The ungodly will face God's judgment. Ungodly can mean irreverent, against God, or simply without God. This word is used four times in verse 15 for emphasis. God will judge the ungodly.

Judgment

Judgment carries with it the conception of right and wrong and punishment for those who do wrong. Judgment is also synonymous with condemnation and damnation.

This idea today is considered politically incorrect, and the masses often reject it. Christians must hold to the truths of Scripture, whether popular or not. The truth of the matter is that God is mankind's Creator and Judge, and He has the right to bless or condemn as He chooses. The ungodly reject these truths and live in their own, self-governing world of their imagined reality. They are "dreamers" (verse 8). Here again, Jude is describing the apostates.

Convict

The Greek word here is *exelencho*, an intensive form of the work *elemcho*. The meaning is "to convict—tell or show someone their faults or to reprove them of their sinful estate—thoroughly."

Ungodly deeds

This is an action, a work that is incomplete and in progress that goes against God and His commandments.

Ungodly way

This is a course of conduct that is against God and His commandments.

Ungodly sinners

This is the fallen condition of man, also translated as offender or debtor who has gone against God and His commandments. God gave us an example of people in the Scriptures who committed ungodly deeds and followed an ungodly way. Their ungodly imitation of Paul brought them to disgrace.

God's miracles done by the hands of Paul were authentic.

> Acts 19:11–12 "Now God worked unusual miracles by the hands of Paul, [12]so that even handkerchiefs or aprons were brought from his body to the sick, and the diseases left them and the evil spirits went out of them."

But some Jewish exorcists took it upon themselves to call upon the name of the Lord Jesus over those who had evil spirits by saying, "We exorcise you by the Jesus whom Paul preaches." They received immediate exposure and humiliation when the man in whom the evil spirit dwelled turned upon them.

> Acts 19:13–15 "Then some of the itinerant Jewish exorcists took it upon themselves to call the name of the Lord Jesus over those who had evil spirits, saying, "We exorcise you by the Jesus whom Paul preaches." [14]Also there were seven sons of Sceva, a Jewish chief priest, who did so. [15]And the evil spirit answered and said, "Jesus I know, and Paul I know; but who are you?" [16]Then the man in whom the evil spirit was leaped on them, overpowered them, and prevailed against them, so that they fled out of that house naked and wounded."

Fear fell upon them all, and those who heard the name of Jesus was magnified. They believed and repented (came confessing and telling of their deeds), and they turned from their wicked ways by burning the books they used for their evil practices, even at the loss of great wealth.

Acts 19:17–19 "This became known both to all Jews and Greeks dwelling in Ephesus; and fear fell on them all, and the name of the LORD Jesus was magnified. [18]And many who had believed came confessing and telling their deeds. [19]Also, many of those who had practiced magic brought their books together and burned them in the sight of all. And they counted up the value of them, and it totaled fifty thousand pieces of silver."

God was glorified, and man was blessed.

Acts 19:20 "So the word of the LORD grew mightily and prevailed."

Sometimes, God may allow ungodly people to expose themselves and receive their just reward right then. But be assured that, when God allows this kind of exposure and punishment, it is for man's good.

God says He hears the harsh things they have spoken against Him. Harsh means unkind, cruel, and, in this case, probably lies and profanities spoken against God.

Ezekiel 35:13–14 "'Thus with your mouth you have boasted against Me and multiplied your words against Me; I have heard them.'"

Life Application Questions

- What does it mean for God to execute judgment?
- Why do you think God used the word "ungodly" four times in verse 15?
- Which tends to happen first, ungodly deeds or an ungodly way?
- How did God bring you to repentance?

VERSE 16

"These are grumblers, complainers, walking according to their own lusts; and they mouth great swelling words, flattering people to gain advantage."

These are grumblers, complainers

Jude is describing how these ungodly men expressed their heart of discontent with God's rule by complaining and grumbling. They complained about their lot and station in the life where God had placed them or allowed them to be. And they grumbled, finding fault with everything, including the blessing and provision of God. There is a warning for grumblers.

> James 5:9 "Do not grumble against one another, brethren, lest you be condemned. Behold the Judge is standing at the door!"

Walking according to their own lusts

The lifestyle and everyday walk of life of these ungodly men, grumblers, and complainers are not according to godliness but are according to the tendencies of their own sinful nature and selfish interests.

And they mouth great swelling words

Swelling words are proud words mouthed flowing from an overinflated ego. This is a graphic description of the ungodly false prophets. They are self-centered and proud. They please only themselves.

2 Peter 2:18. "For when they speak great swelling words of emptiness, the allure through the lusts of the flesh, through lewdness, the ones who have actually escaped from those who live in error."

Flattering people to gain advantage

This means manipulative, speaking with the wrong motives. We can bless others by letting them know how much they mean to us. But Jude reveals here that one of the characteristics of the apostate is that he compliments or flatters only to his own advantage. The apostate's motives are all wrong. He is manipulative. Even the things he says that seem to be good and complimentary are only for his wicked, selfish plans.

Paul, an example for us, was about setting the world right side up. The apostates are about setting the world upside down. What apostates do is in total opposition to Paul's motives and approach to the work God had called him to do. Paul spoke only the Truth and suffered as he carried the Truth, just as Christ had suffered. Paul set a good example, even though he personally gained no advantage. Paul's example shows us to follow Christ in spreading the Truth and to allow God to work and direct.

In the following Scripture, the Jews were about following an ungodly way, seeking to turn the world upside down so darkness would fall upon man. The Jews in Thessalonica used their professed allegiance to Caesar to make hostile accusations against Paul, the other missionaries, and the brethren in Jason's house who accepted and believed the teachings of Paul. This ungodly behavior disrupted the preaching of Christ in Thessalonica. Serving God came at a cost. Jason and the brethren served in the discord and disruption created by the hostile Jews and even had to pay bail to regain their freedom.

Acts 17:5–9 "But the Jews who were not persuaded, becoming envious, took some of the evil men from the marketplace, and gathering a mob, set all the city in an uproar and attacked the house of Jason, and sought to bring them out to the people. ⁶But when they did not find them, they dragged Jason and some brethren to the rulers of the city, crying out, "These who have turned the world upside down have come here too. ⁷Jason has harbored them, and these are all acting contrary to the decrees of Caesar, saying there is another king—Jesus." ⁸And they troubled the crowd and the rulers of the city when they heard these things. ⁹So when they had taken security from Jason and the rest, they let them go."

But God, in His manner of doing things, set things right and used it for His glory and the blessing of man.

Acts 17:10–12 "Then the brethren immediately sent Paul and Silas away by night to Berea. When they arrived, they went into the synagogue of the Jews. ¹¹These were more fair-minded than those in Thessalonica, in that they received the word with all readiness, and searched the Scriptures daily to find out whether these things were so. ¹²Therefore many of them believed, and also not a few of the Greeks, prominent women as well as men."

Continuing to show the fullness of the incident, Paul also speaks of how God was able to use this incident of the unbelieving Jews at Thessalonica and the good example of the Christian Thessalonians as witness that brought people to God in his first letter to the Thessalonians.

1 Thessalonians 1:6–9 "And you became followers of us and of the LORD, having received the word in much affliction, with joy of the Holy Spirit, ⁷so that you became examples to all in Macedonia and Achaia who believe. ⁸For from you the

word of the LORD has sounded forth, not only in Macedonia and Achaia, but also in every place. Your faith toward God has gone out, so that we do not need to say anything. [9]For they themselves declare concerning us what manner of entry we had to you, and how you turned to God from idols to serve the living and true God,"

The Jews from Thessalonica wouldn't give up their ungodly ways and even followed Paul to Berea to stir up the people.

> Acts 17:13 "But when the Jews from Thessalonica learned that the word of God was preached by Paul at Berea, they came there also and stirred up the crowds."

And God used this to send Paul and the missionaries on to Athens, where Paul faced another challenge. He saw that the city was given over to idols.

> Acts 17:16 "Now while Paul waited for them at Athens, his spirit was provoked within him when he saw that the city was given over to idols."

Paul presented the gospel. He spoke of how God had overlooked the religious ignorance of the people but explained the Truth had come to dwell among them. Paul preached the Truth. Some mocked, but some were added to the number of missionaries.

> Acts 17:31–34 "because He (GOD) has appointed a day on which He will judge the world in righteousness by the Man whom He has ordained. He has given assurance of this to all by raising Him from the dead. [32]And when they heard of the resurrection of the dead, some mocked, while others said, "We will hear you again on this matter." [33]So Paul departed from among them. [34]However, some men joined him and

believed, among them Dionysius the Areopagite, a woman named Damaris, and others with them."

Paul faced the false teachers and the apostates, did what God called him to do, and allowed God to handle the rest.

Life Application Questions

- What does it mean to "mouth" great swelling words?
- How does this apply to your life?
- What advantage(s) are these men, who both Jude and Paul speak of, seeking to gain?
- Has there been a time in your life when you saw God use someone who was following an ungodly way to bring people to Himself?

VERSE 17

"But you, beloved, remember the words which were spoken before by the apostles of our LORD Jesus Christ:"

But you

This is a direct address to the readers of Jude. Jude makes a clear distinction between the ungodly men he has been writing about and his readers. He has been addressing the problem of ungodly men who are apostate concerning the true faith.

Jude has given much attention to describe the characteristics of these certain ungodly men who have crept in among the fellowship of true believers (verse 4). And now twice in four verses, Jude says, "But you . . ." (verse 17 and 20). There is a clear and distinct contrast between the true and false Christians. We are called to actively pay attention to this difference.

Beloved

The Greek word is *agapetos* (*ag-ap-ay-tos*). This particular form of the Greek word *agapao* (*ag-ap-ah'-o*), esteemed or favorite, often used in the New Testament to describe the kind of love God displays, is found only here in the book of Jude. This is the attitude God has toward us and the attitude we should have toward one another.

Remember

This means to look back, recall, and think on. One of the most important things we as Christians will ever do is remember. Christianity is not that complicated. Even though the rules and principles of our faith are really quite simple, we forget them. One of the greatest dangers a Christian faces is forgetfulness. We forget the great lessons God has clearly taught us. We forget the ugliness of sin. And we forget and lose sight of Jesus, our first love. We lose focus and let worldly distractions overtake our vision. We take our eyes off God, and our field of vision becomes distorted.

Forgetting is absentmindedly or purposefully not remembering. It is the opposite of remembering.

> Revelation 2:4–5 (Jesus speaking) "Nevertheless I have this against you, that you have left your first love. [5]Remember therefore from where you have fallen; repent and do the first works, or else I will come to you quickly and remove your lampstand from its place—unless you repent."

> James 1:23–24 "For if anyone is a hearer of the Word and not a doer, he is like a man who looks at his natural face in a mirror; [24]for once he has looked at himself and gone away, he has immediately forgotten what kind of person he was."

This is why we must devote ourselves continually to fellowship and the studying of God's Word with a true heart in the full assurance of faith as you see the day approaching.

> Acts 2:42 "And they continued steadfastly in the apostles' doctrine and fellowship, in the breaking of bread, and in prayers,"

Hebrews 10:15–25 "But the Holy Spirit also witnesses to us; for after He had said before, [16]"This is the covenant that I will make with them after those days, says the LORD: I will put My laws into their hearts, and in their minds I will write them," [17]then He adds, "Their sins and their lawless deeds I will remember no more." [18]Now where there is remission of these, there is no longer an offering for sin. [19]Therefore, brethren, having boldness to enter the Holiest by the blood of Jesus, [20]by a new and living way which He consecrated for us, through the veil, that is, His flesh, [21]and having a High Priest over the house of God, [22]let us draw near with a true heart in full assurance of faith, having our hearts sprinkled from an evil conscience and our bodies washed with pure water. [23]Let us hold fast the confession of our hope without wavering, for He who promised is faithful." [24]And let us consider one another in order to stir up love and good works, [25]not forsaking the assembling of ourselves together, as is the manner of some, but exhorting one another, and so much the more as you see the Day approaching."

The words which were spoken before by the apostles of our LORD Jesus Christ

These are spoken before in the New Testament as well as the Old Testament. The words spoken of here are God's Word to us.

1 Thessalonians 2:13 "For this reason we also thank God without ceasing, because when you received the word of God which you heard from us, you welcomed it not as the word of men, but as it is in truth, the word of God which also effectively works in you who believed."

Life Application Questions

- Why did Jude address his readers with "but you" at the beginning of this passage?
- What are some things that help us to remember and act upon the things of God?
- What do you need to do to allow the words of God, spoken and written by the apostles of our LORD Jesus Christ, to effectively work in you?

Verse 18

"How they told you that there would be mockers in the last time who would walk according to their own ungodly lusts."

How they told you that there would be mockers

They, the apostles, have posted warning; there will be mockers or scoffers. Mockers are those who act in an immature offensive, an ungodly way. They deride and sneer at the target of their mocking. They mock the commands of God by walking in their own way, in their own ungodly lusts, instead of living God's way. They are also called scoffers. Some who are mockers covet and deceive, sometimes for financial gain. Others may be a mocker to gain followers.

> 2 Peter 2:2–3 "And many will follow their destructive ways, because of whom the way of truth will be blasphemed. ³By covetousness they will exploit you with deceptive words; for a long time their judgment has not been idle, and their destruction does not slumber."

Jesus was mocked.

> Matthew 27:29–31, "When they had twisted a crown of thorns, they put it on His head, and a reed in His right hand, And they bowed the knee before Him and mocked Him, saying, 'Hail, King of the Jews!' ³⁰Then they spat on Him, and took the reed and struck Him on the head. ³¹And when

they had mocked Him, they took the robe off Him, put His own clothes on him, and led Him away to be crucified."

They continued to mock Him by asking Him to demonstrate His power and save Himself from the pain and agony of the cross. They did not know or did not accept the plan of God to reveal His power in His time in His way.

Matthew 27:40 "and saying, You who destroy the temple and build it in three days, save Yourself! If you are the Son of God, come down from the cross."

Mark 15:29–30 "And those who passed by blasphemed Him, wagging their heads and saying, 'Aha! You who destroy the temple and build it in three day, ³⁰save Yourself, and come down from the cross!'"

Jesus' followers have been and will be mocked, just as Jesus was.

Hebrews 11:36 "Still others had trial of mockings and scourgings, yes and of chains and imprisonment."

Isaiah speaks of the result of mockery. Judah (Isaiah speaks here of just the tribe of Judah, not the Jews as a whole) mocked God by putting their faith in human leadership, walking in an ungodly way instead of God's way. Their leadership became weaker and weaker. They brought about their own destruction by not following God's way.

Isaiah 3:4–5 "I will give children to be their princes and babes shall rule over them ⁵The people will be oppressed, Every one by another and every one by his neighbor; The child will be insolent toward the elder and the base toward the honorable."

106

Scripture says God is not mocked. There are consequences.

> Galatians 6:7–8 "Do not be deceived, God is not mocked;
> for whatever a man sows, that he will also reap [8]For he who
> sows to his flesh will of the flesh reap corruption, but he who
> sows to the Spirit will of the Spirit reap everlasting life."

In the last time

The last times begin when Jesus, the Gospel "comes alive," came to Earth. The last time begins a time when the Gospel would be preached to the entire world.

> Matthew 24:14 "And this gospel of the kingdom will be
> preached in all the world as a witness to all the nations, and
> then the end will come" (See also Matthew 24–25.)

> Mark 13:33, 37 "Take heed, watch and pray; for you do not
> know when the time is. [37]And what I say to you, I say to all:
> Watch!" (See also Mark 13–14.)

> Luke 21:34–36 "But take heed to yourselves, lest your
> hearts be weighted down with carousing, drunkenness, and
> cares of this life, and that Day come on you unexpectedly.
> [35]For it will come as a snare on all those who dwell on
> the face of the whole earth. [36]Watch therefore, and pray
> always that you may be counted worthy to escape all these
> things that will come to pass and to stand before the Son
> of Man."

When the development of God's plan of salvation ends, there will come a time of final and decisive judgment, the end of God's timetable for mankind on Earth as we know it.

2 Timothy 3:1 "But know this, that in the last days perilous times will come:"

1 John 2:18 "Little children, it is the last hour; and as you have heard that the Antichrist is coming, even now may antichrists have come, by which we know that is the last hour."

The antichrist will come at the end of the age and claim the loyalty due to Christ. The opposition will take many forms, but they will have one thing in common. They will not have accepted the gift of salvation through Jesus Christ, and they will deny the humanity and deity of Jesus. God tells us what will come to pass in the last days.

Acts 2:17 "And it shall come to pass in the last days, says God, that I will pour out of My Spirit on all flesh; your sons and your daughters shall prophesy, your young men shall see visions, your old men shall dream dreams."

False teaching will increase because people want to hear what pleases them rather than what is the scriptural truth.

2 Timothy 4:3 "For the time will come when they will not endure sound doctrine, but according to their own desires, because they have itching ear, they will heap up for themselves teachers."

But God has spoken to us through His Son.

Hebrews 1:1–2 "Has in these last days spoken to us by His Son, whom He has appointed heir of all things, through whom also He made the worlds;"

Be not deceived these things will come to pass.

Matthew 24:4–6 "And Jesus answered and said to them: '(Jesus speaking) Take heed that no one deceives you. ⁵ For many will come in My name, saying, "I am the Christ" and will deceive many. ⁶And you will hear of wars and rumors of wars. See that you are not troubled; for all these things must come to ass, but the end is not yet.'"

There is comfort for us in the last times.

1 Thessalonians 4:16–18 "For the LORD Himself will descend from heaven with a shout, with the voice of an archangel, and with the trumpet of God. And the dead in Christ will rise first. ¹⁷Then we who are alive and remain shall be caught up together with them in the clouds to meet the LORD in the air. And this we shall always be with the LORD. ¹⁸Therefore comfort one another with these words."

Who would walk according to their own ungodly lusts

"Walk according" means living as if God were not the creator of the world and as if the world were not dependent on God. "Ungodly lusts" are fleshly desires that are not God planned or directed, nor are they according to His laws. The teachings of Jesus and the apostles included warnings of the coming of false prophets, ungodly men, lovers of self, and God mockers or scoffers.

Matthew 24:11 "Then many false prophets will rise up and deceive many."

Acts 20:29 "For I know this, that after my departure savage wolves will come in among you not sparing the flock."

1 Timothy 4:1–2 "Now the Spirit expressly says that in latter times some will depart from the faith, giving heed to

deceiving spirits and doctrines of demons, [2]speaking lies in hypocrisy, having their own conscience seared with a hot iron."

2 Timothy 3:2–5 "For men will be lovers of themselves, lovers of money, boasters, proud, blasphemers, disobedient to parents, unthankful, unholy, [3]unloving, unforgiving, slanderers, without self-control, brutal, despisers of good, [4]traitors, headstrong, haughty, lovers of pleasure rather than lovers of God, [5]having a form of godliness but denying its power. And from such people turn away!"

2 Peter 2:1 "But there were also false prophets among the people, even as there will be false teachers among you, who will secretly bring in destructive heresies, even denying the LORD who bought them, and bring on themselves swift destruction."

2 Peter 3:3–7 "Knowing this first: that scoffers will come in the last days, walking according to their own lusts, [4]and saying, "Where is the promise of His (Jesus) coming? For since the fathers fell asleep, all things continue as they were from the beginning of creation." [5]For this they willfully forget: that by the word of God the heavens were of old, and the earth standing out of water and in the water, [6]by which the world that then existed perished, being flooded with water. [7]But the heavens and the earth which are now preserved by the same word, are reserved for fire until the Day of Judgment and perdition of ungodly men."

We have been instructed and warned throughout God's Word.

Galatians 5:13 "For you were called to freedom, brethren; only do not turn your freedom into an opportunity for the flesh, but through love serve one another."

Life Application Questions

- What are mockers?
- What does "the last time" mean in the context of this verse?
- What does "the last time" mean in the context of your life and how you live it?

VERSE 19

"These are sensual persons, who cause divisions, not having the Spirit."

These are sensual persons

The word "sensual" is not restricted to sexual desires. Sensual refers to all the natural desires of the flesh. Natural desires of the flesh include bitter envy, self-seeking, greed, self-preservation, a desire to elevate oneself, covetousness, being desirous of vain glory, and idolatry. Jude makes a distinction between those who would live according to the flesh and its desires and those who live according to the Spirit. This distinction is further explained in Paul's writing to the Romans.

> Romans 8:4–16 "That the righteous requirement of the law might be fulfilled in us who do not walk according to the flesh but according to the Spirit. ⁵For those who live according to the flesh set their minds on the things of the flesh, but those who live according to the Spirit, the things of the Spirit. ⁶For to be carnally minded is death, but to be spiritually minded is life and peace. ⁷Because the carnal mind is enmity against God; for it is not subject to the law of God, nor indeed can be. ⁸So then, those who are in the flesh cannot please God. ⁹But you are not in the flesh but in the Spirit, if indeed the Spirit of God dwells in you. Now if anyone does not have the Spirit of Christ, he is not His. ¹⁰And if Christ is in you, the body is dead because of sin,

but the Spirit is life because of righteousness. [11]But if the Spirit of Him who raised Jesus from the dead dwells in you, He who raised Christ from the dead will also give life to your mortal bodies through His Spirit who dwells in you. [12]Therefore, brethren, we are debtors—not to the flesh, to live according to the flesh. [13]For if you live according to the flesh you will die; but if by the Spirit you put to death the deeds of the body, you will live. [14]For as many as are led by the Spirit of God, these are sons of God. [15]For you did not receive the spirit of bondage again to fear, but you received the Spirit of adoption by whom we cry out, "Abba, Father." [16]The Spirit Himself bears witness with our spirit that we are children of God,"

Who cause divisions

One of the many negative characteristics of a sensual person who lives according to his flesh rather than being led by God's Spirit is that he is divisive. Those who live according to the flesh bring division by their manipulative and selfish ways. A selfish self-serving person would naturally promote division in the body of Christ because the person who lives by his flesh cannot be living by the word of God. See Romans 8:6–7 above. They are as far apart as death and life.

A person cannot live to serve both God and self. A house divided will fall.

> Matthew 12:25 (Jesus speaking) "But Jesus knew their thoughts and said to them: 'Every kingdom divided against itself is brought to desolation, and every city or house divided against itself will not stand.'"

This is also stated in Luke 11:17. James also speaks about those who are double-minded (divided).

James 4:1–10 "Where do wars and fights come from among you? Do they not come from your desires for pleasure that war in your members? ²You lust and do not have. You murder and covet and cannot obtain. You fight and war. Yet you do not have because you do not ask. ³You ask and do not receive, because you ask amiss, that you may spend it on your pleasures. ⁴Adulterers and adulteresses! Do you not know that friendship with the world is enmity with God? Whoever therefore wants to be a friend of the world makes himself an enemy of God. ⁵Or do you think that the Scripture says in vain, "The Spirit who dwells in us yearns jealously"? ⁶But He gives more grace. Therefore He says: 'God resists the proud, but gives grace to the humble.' ⁷Therefore submit to God. Resist the devil and he will flee from you. ⁸Draw near to God and He will draw near to you. Cleanse your hands, you sinners; and purify your hearts, you double-minded. ⁹Lament and mourn and weep! Let your laughter be turned to mourning and your joy to gloom. ¹⁰Humble yourselves in the sight of the Lord, and He will lift you up."

To lament, mourn, and weep is the right attitude toward unfaithfulness.

We must pay attention. The Holy Spirit of God leads the children of God to be submissive, accommodating, and loving to one another. The work of the Holy Spirit in Christians promotes unity of the brethren, and unity is God's plan for His children.

1 Peter 3:8 "Finally, all of you be of one mind, having compassion for one another; love as brothers, be tenderhearted, be courteous."

Romans 15:5–6 "Now may the God of patience and comfort grant you to be like-minded toward one another, according to Jesus Christ, ⁶That you may with one mind and one mouth glorify the God and Father of our LORD Jesus Christ."

Not having the Spirit

This means devoid of the Spirit of God. Without the Holy Spirit of God governing a person's life, you cannot expect anything but sensuality and what comes naturally to the carnal nature.

> 1 Corinthians 2:14 "But the natural man does not receive the things of the Spirit of God, for they are foolishness to him; nor can he know them, because they are spiritually discerned."

> James 3:13–15 "Who is wise and understanding among you? Let him show by good conduct that his works are done in the meekness of wisdom ¹⁴But if you have bitter envy and self-seeking in your hearts do not boast and lie against the truth. ¹⁵This wisdom does not descend from above, but is earthly, sensual, demonic."

Life Application Questions

- What are "sensual persons"?
- Where does wisdom that is "not from above" come from?
- How are we to handle such "wisdom"?

Verse 20

"But you, beloved, building yourselves up on your most holy faith, praying in the Holy Spirit,"

But you, beloved

Again, Jude reminds us, but you, Christian readers who are led by the Holy Spirit and beloved of God, are called and sanctified (*hagiazzo*) and set apart living in the fullness of the love of God. (Beloved is in contrast to those who are caught up in worldly pursuits.)

> 2 Thessalonians 2:13–14 "But we are bound to give thanks to God always for you, brethren beloved by the LORD, because God from the beginning chose you for salvation through sanctification by the Spirit and belief in the truth. [14]to which He called you by our gospel, for the obtaining of the glory of our LORD Jesus Christ."

Building yourselves up on your most holy faith

Christians are to build themselves up in the faith. Some determine that this would be entirely up to God and His providence. But Jude and the other writers of the New Testament indicate otherwise. God wants us to be spiritually healthy. In order to become spiritually healthy, you are to build yourselves up in the faith.

"The faith" may be defined as the body of truth that you, as Christians, are to learn so you may live a holy life. It is holy because it is from God, and God is holy.

1 Peter 1:15–16 "but as He who called you is holy, you also be holy in all your conduct, ¹⁶because it is written 'Be holy, for I am holy.'"

"Building yourselves up in the faith" is a step-by-step process that begins with salvation.

2 Thessalonians 2:13–14 "But we are bound to give thanks to God always for you brethren beloved by the Lord, because God from the beginning chose you for salvation through sanctification by the Spirit and belief in the truth ¹⁴to which He called you by our gospel for the obtaining of the glory of our Lord Jesus Christ."

Your foundation for the building of faith (the acceptance, belief, and living out of a life governed by the Truth) must be built on the rock of Jesus Christ (Matthew 7:24–27). You must be born again by water and the Spirit (John 3:5–8). As you seek first the kingdom of God (Matthew 6:33) and His righteousness, the Spirit works within you to bring about the changes needed in order for you to live and enjoy the fullness of God's blessing (Ephesians 3:14–21).

The process of sanctification is preparation for your journey into glory that you may spend eternity with the Lord and enter his rest (Revelations 14:13). This process is worked out as you submit, trust, and obey (Philippians 2:12–13) and put off your former conduct (Ephesians. 4:22). The word of God and the work of the Holy Spirit brings about the renewal of your minds and transformation into the likeness of Jesus (Romans 12:2, Ephesians. 4:23–24).

The Christian faith is "most holy." These two words come from one Greek word, *hagios* (*hag'-ee-os*), meaning "set apart." This same Greek word is translated "saints" sixty-one times in the New Testament, referring to all true Christians. The true Christian is to be holy and set apart, actively exercising self-discipline and building himself or herself up in the faith.

A part of the process of building yourself up in the faith is to walk circumspectly to redeem your time from the evil ways of today.

> Ephesians 5:15–20 "See then that you walk circumspectly, not as fools but as wise, [16]redeeming the time, because the days are evil. [17]Therefore do not be unwise, but understand what the will of the LORD is [18]And do not be drunk with wine, in which is dissipation; but be filled with the Spirit,"

You are to worship and give thanks.

> Ephesians 5:19–20 "speaking to one another in psalms and hymns and spiritual songs, singing and making melody in your heart to the LORD, [20]giving thanks always for all things to God the Father in the name of our LORD Jesus Christ."

You are to study God's Word to prepare to be a kingdom worker who does not have to be ashamed and is able to rightly handle the word of Truth.

> 2 Timothy 2:15 "Be diligent to present yourself approved to God, a worker who does not need to be ashamed, rightly dividing the word of truth."

Daily disciplines for building yourself in the faith include the following:

- **Prayer:**
  1 Thessalonians 5:17 "Pray without ceasing."

- **Forgiveness, forgiving, and being forgiven:**
  Matthew 6:14–15 "For if you forgive men their trespasses, your heavenly Father will also forgive you. [15]but if you do

not forgive men their trespasses, neither will your Father forgive your trespasses."

- **Allowing His Spirit to strengthen your inner man:**

  Ephesians 3:16 "That He would grant you, according to the riches of His glory, to be strengthened with might through His Spirit in the inner man,"

- **Acting honorably:**

  2 Corinthians 13:7 "Now I pray to God that you do no evil, not that we should appear approved, but that you should do what is honorable, though we may seem disqualified."

- **Love (accepting being loved and loving):**

  1 John 3:17–19 "But whoever has this world's goods, and sees his brother in need, and shuts up his heart from him, how does the love of God abide in him. [18]My little children, let us not love in word or in tongue, but in deed and in truth [19]And by this we know that we are of the truth, and shall assure our hearts before Him."

  Hebrews 13:1–2 "Let brotherly love continue. [2]Do not forget to entertain strangers, for by so doing some have unwittingly entertained angels."

  1 John 4:7–8 "Beloved, let us love one another for love is of God; and everyone who loves is born of God and knows God. [8]He who does not love does not know God, for God is love."

  Deuteronomy 6:4–5 "Hear, O Israel: The LORD our God, the LORD is one! [5]You shall love the LORD your God with all your heart, with all your soul, and with all your strength."

2 Timothy 1:7 "For God has not given us a spirit of fear, but of power and of love and of a sound mind."

- **Practicing stewardship:**

  Matthew 25:21 "His LORD said to him, 'Well done good and faithful servant; you were faithful over a few things, I will make you ruler over many things. Enter into the joy of your LORD.'"

  1 Corinthians 4:1–2 "Let a man so consider us, as servants of Christ and stewards of the mysteries of God. ²Morever it is required in stewards that one be found faithful."

- **Sharing your faith:**

  Philemon 1:6 "That the sharing of your faith may become effective by the acknowledgment of every good thing which is in you in Christ Jesus."

- **Holding fast to the good (the standard for good, the Ten Commandments):**

  1 Thessalonians 5:21 "Test all things; hold fast what is good."

- **Fellowshipping with the saints and holding one another accountable:**

  Hebrews 10:24–25 "And let us consider one another in order to stir up love and good works, ²⁵not forsaking the assembling of ourselves together, as is the manner of some, but exhorting one another, and so much the more as you see the Day approaching."

  Acts 2:42 "They continued steadfastly in the apostles' doctrine and fellowship, in the breaking of bread, and in prayers."

2 Peter 1:5–12 "But also for this very reason, giving all diligence, add to your faith virtue, to virtue knowledge, [6]to knowledge self-control, to self-control perseverance, to perseverance godliness, [7]to godliness brotherly kindness, and to brotherly kindness love. [8]For if these things are yours and abound, you will be neither barren nor unfruitful in the knowledge of our LORD Jesus Christ. [9]For he who lacks these things is shortsighted, even to blindness, and has forgotten that he was cleansed from his old sins. [10]Therefore, brethren, be even more diligent to make your call and election sure, for if you do these things you will never stumble; [11]for so an entrance will be supplied to you abundantly into the everlasting kingdom of our LORD and Savior Jesus Christ. [12]For this reason I will not be negligent to remind you always of these things, though you know and are established in the present truth."

- **Accepting the invitation to come and rest:**
  Matthew 11:28–30 "Come to Me all you who labor and are heavy laden, and I will give you rest. [29]Take My yoke upon you and learn from Me, for I am gentle and lowly in heart, and you will find rest for you souls. [30]For My yoke is easy and My burden is light."

This study on building the faith would not be complete without a look at the faith teaching in Hebrews. This begins in Hebrews 10:19 and continues through Hebrews 11. The patriarchs believed God's promises, and by faith, exercising self-discipline, and building themselves up in the faith, they became overcomers. This faithful cloud of witnesses surrounds us, and we have also received even more than them, the promise of salvation in Jesus, our example.

Hebrews 12:1–2 "Therefore we also, since we are surrounded by so great a cloud of witnesses, let us lay aside every weight, and the sin which so easily ensnares us, and let us run with endurance the race that is set before us, ²looking unto Jesus, the author and finisher of our faith, who for the joy that was set before Him endured the cross, despising the shame, and has sat down at the right hand of the throne of God."

But some of God's chosen people could not enter His rest because of unbelief.

Hebrews 3:16–19 "For who, having heard, rebelled? Indeed, was it not all who came out of Egypt, led by Moses? ¹⁷Now with whom was He angry forty years? Was it not with those who sinned, whose corpses fell in the wilderness? ¹⁸And to whom did He swear that they would not enter His rest, but to those who did not obey? ¹⁹So we see that they could not enter in because of unbelief."

But the promise of entering His rest remained.

Hebrews 4:1–3 "Therefore, since a promise remains of entering His rest, let us fear lest any of you seem to have come short of it. ²For indeed the gospel was preached to us as well as to them; but the word which they heard did not profit them, not being mixed with faith in those who heard it. ³For we who have believed do enter that rest, as He has said: 'So I swore in My wrath, They shall not enter My rest,' although the works were finished from the foundation of the world."

Godly fruits are a natural outgrowth of the learning process as you build yourself up in the faith and the Truth becomes real in your life. As the Truth lives in you, you are able to turn from your selfish and evil ways to walk in the ways of your Father, God. Self-control is a fruit of the spirit by which you demonstrate the work of the Holy Spirit within you.

> Galatians 5:22–23 "But the fruit of the Spirit is love, joy, peace, longsuffering, kindness, goodness, faithfulness, [23]gentleness, self-control. Against such there is no law."

By faith, go in peace.

> Luke 7:50 (Jesus speaking) "Your faith has saved you, Go in peace."

Readers we exhort you, just as Paul exhorted the Ephesian elders.

> Acts 20:32 "So now, brethren, I commend you to God and to the Word of His grace, which is able to build you up and give you an inheritance among all those who are sanctified.

Praying in the Holy Spirit

The Scriptures teach that, in the limited understanding of our fleshly minds, we don't even know how to pray as we should. We need the Holy Spirit of God to lead us in our prayers.

> Romans 8:26–27 "Likewise the Spirit also helps in our weaknesses. For we do not know what we should pray for as we ought, but the Spirit Himself makes intercession for us with groanings which cannot be uttered. [27]Now He who searches the hearts knows what the mind of the Spirit is, because He makes intercession for the saints according to the will of God."

Life Application Questions

- Why do Christians need to walk circumspectly?
- Why are Christians supposed to study God's Word?
- How are you exercising self-discipline so you may be "building yourself up in the faith"? What more can you do?
- How does the Holy Spirit help us to pray?

Verse 21

"Keep yourselves in the love of God, looking for the mercy of our LORD Jesus Christ unto eternal life."

Keep yourselves in the love of God

This means to intentionally make all efforts to remain in the steadfast love of God. Be careful not to misunderstand this command. God already loves us, and we need do nothing to keep His love.

> Romans 8:35–39 "Who shall separate us from the love of Christ? Shall tribulation, or distress, or persecution, or famine, or nakedness, or peril, or sword? [36]As it is written: "For Your sake we are killed all day long; we are accounted as sheep for the slaughter" (Psalms 44:22) [37]Yet in all these things we are more than conquerors through Him who loved us. [38]For I am persuaded that neither death nor life, nor angels nor principalities nor powers, nor things present nor things to come, [39]nor height nor depth, nor any other created thing, shall be able to separate us from the love of God which is in Christ Jesus our LORD."

We can choose to think or act outside of the influence of His love. Every Christian has the responsibility to be led by the Holy Spirit of God and live within the will and love of God. It is our free will choice. For some examples of this, see the book of John.

> John 15:9–10 (Jesus speaking) "As the Father loved Me, I also have loved you; abide in My love. ¹⁰If you keep My commandments, you will abide in My love, just as I have kept My Father's commandments and abide in His love."

The Father's love for the Son is the measure of Christ's love for us. We abide in His love when we keep his commandments.

> Acts 11:23 "When he (Barnabas) came and had seen the grace of God, he was glad, and encouraged them all that with purpose of heart they should continue with the LORD."

The church in Jerusalem sent Barnabas to Antioch to see firsthand if what they were hearing from Antioch was true of the Gentile converts. If what he were hearing was true, he was to encourage them in their faith. Remember, he was the one who encouraged Saul early.

> 1 John 5:21 "Little children, keep yourselves from idols."

Idols probably refer to teaching that is contrary to Scripture, particularly teaching that denies the full deity and humanity of Jesus. We are to guard diligently against any false understanding, teaching.

Just as we are each personally responsible to "build ourselves up in our most holy faith" (verse 20), we are also personally responsible to "keep ourselves in the love of God." This is a command to live according to God's love and its work in our lives.

Looking for the mercy of our LORD Jesus Christ

This completes the command to "keep ourselves in the love of God." This attitude helps keep the Christian focused and on track. Christians should be looking for the mercy of the LORD. Mercy is the view of God's kindness rather than of His judgment. We are certainly told in

Scripture to be aware that we shall all stand before the judgment seat of Christ

> Romans 14:10 "But why do you judge your brother? Or why do you show contempt for your brother? For we shall all stand before the judgment seat of Christ."

> 2 Corinthians 5:10 "For we must all appear before the judgment seat of Christ, that each one may receive the things done in the body, according to what he has done, whether good or bad."

"Done in the body" is what we did before our salvation.

But even at that time of judgment, if we are keeping ourselves in the love of God, our expectation on that day is mercy and not condemnation.

> 1 John 3:2 "Beloved, now we are children of God and it has not yet been revealed what we shall be, but we know that when He is revealed, we shall be like Him, for we shall see Him as He is."

This gives the believer a future and a hope. Peter had this mind-set when he wrote the following.

> 1 Peter 1:13 "Therefore gird up the loins of your mind, be sober, and rest your hope fully upon the grace that is to be brought to you at the revelation of Jesus Christ."

In Peter's time, people had to gather up the long robes they wore in order to be free to do anything energetic. Today, we say, "Roll up your shirtsleeves." Both mean we are to be ready for mental and spiritual activity.

Unto eternal life

This means life everlasting, forever. People will spend eternity somewhere determined by the choices they make as they live out their earthly existence.

Another thing Christians sometimes forget is their future. Christians will live eternally with God in heaven. When you lose perspective of your eternity, you tend to put too high of a priority upon the temporary activities of this life. Eternal life is a life unending. But more importantly, it is a life of knowing God through Jesus.

> John 17:3 "And this is eternal life, that they may know You, the only true God, and Jesus Christ whom You have sent."

Life Application Questions

- What does it mean to "keep yourself in the love of God"?
- What does it mean to act outside the influence of God's love?
- How has the mercy of God affected your life?
- What gives you a future and a hope?

Verse 22

"And on some have compassion, making a distinction;"

And on some have compassion

Compassion means to have an attitude of mercy and being willing to come alongside to help. Jude is indicating that we should not treat all those who are in error the same. We need discernment that the Holy Spirit might lead us to know whether the particular person we are dealing with needs comfort, rebuke, or enlightenment, that is, Truth applied.

But there are some who, if they were only shown the truth in the Scriptures, would turn to the true faith. Christians are called to minister to the least of these. These people especially need God's mercy and compassion poured through us in the hope that they would be able to accept the truth.

Making a distinction

This means to lovingly discriminate according to discernment. We are to exercise godly wisdom in making a distinction about approaching some people and some circumstances. First, we must make sure that God has called us and is leading us. In carrying out this work, we are called to:

- **Love:**
  John 15:12 (Jesus speaking) "This is My commandment, that you love one another as I have loved you."

- **Keep His commandments:**

  John 14:15–17 (Jesus speaking) "If you love Me, keep My commandments. [16]And I will pray the Father, and He will give you another Helper, that He may abide with you forever—[17]the Spirit of truth, whom the world cannot receive, because it neither sees Him nor knows Him; but you know Him, for He dwells with you and will be in you."

- **Speak the truth in love:**

  Ephesians 4:15–16 "but, speaking the truth in love, may grow up in all things unto Him who is the head—Christ—[16]from whom the whole body, joined and knit together by what every joint supplies according to the effective working by which every part does its share, causes growth of the body for the edifying of itself in love."

- **Hold fast to the sound doctrine we have been given:**

  2 Timothy 1:13–14 "Hold fast the pattern of sound words which you have heard from me, in faith and love which are in Christ Jesus. [14]That good thing which was committed to you, keep by the Holy Spirit who dwells in us."

Second, we must prepare and allow God to give us what is needed for the task.

Romans 12:1–3 "I beseech you therefore, brethren, by the mercies of God, that you present your bodies a living sacrifice, holy, acceptable to God, which is your reasonable service. [2]And do not be conformed to this world, but be transformed by the renewing of your mind, that you may prove what is that good and acceptable and perfect will of God. [3]For I say, through the grace given to me, to everyone who is among you, not to think of himself more highly than he ought to think, but to think soberly, as God has dealt to each one a measure of faith."

Our instructions are found in Romans.

Romans 12:14–17 "Bless those who persecute you; bless and do not curse. [15]Rejoice with those who rejoice, and weep with those who weep. [16]Be of the same mind toward one another. Do not set your mind on high things, but associate with the humble. Do not be wise in your own opinion.[17]Repay no one evil for evil. Have regard for good things in the sight of all men."

We are called to be imitators of God, walk in love, and bring the light.

Ephesians 5:1–13 "Therefore be imitators of God as dear children. [2]And walk in love, as Christ also has loved us and given Himself for us, an offering and a sacrifice to God for a sweet-smelling aroma. [3]But fornication and all uncleanness or covetousness, let it not even be named among you, as is fitting for saints; [4]neither filthiness, nor foolish talking, nor coarse jesting, which are not fitting, but rather giving of thanks. [5]For this you know, that no fornicator, unclean person, nor covetous man, who is an idolater, has any inheritance in the kingdom of Christ and God. [6]Let no one deceive you with empty words, for because of these things the wrath of God comes upon the sons of disobedience. [7]Therefore do not be partakers with them. [8]For you were once darkness, but now you are light in the LORD. Walk as children of light [9](for the fruit of the Spirit is in all goodness, righteousness, and truth), [10]finding out what is acceptable to the LORD. [11]And have no fellowship with the unfruitful works of darkness, but rather expose them. [12]For it is shameful even to speak of those things which are done by them in secret. [13]But all things that are exposed are made manifest by the light, for whatever makes manifest is light."

In order to make a distinction, we need discernment so we might know how each individual should be treated. We should work in the full knowledge that only God fully knows his or her heart and motive. When we seek discernment, God will give us understanding and wisdom.

> Proverbs 2:3–6 "Yes, if you cry out for discernment, And lift up your voice for understanding, [4]If you seek her as silver, And search for her as for hidden treasures: [5]Then you will understand the fear of the LORD, And find the knowledge of God. [6]For the LORD gives wisdom: From His mouth come knowledge and understanding:"

God communicates to us through His Word and the Holy Spirit, which He sent to live in us at the moment of our salvation. The work of the Holy Spirit is to bring us to deeper understanding of God's Word and our environment. This deeper understanding is given for the profit of all we might carry out our assignment. This includes making a distinction for the work of the kingdom.

> 1 Corinthians 12:7 "But the manifestation of the Spirit is given to each one for the profit of all:"

The Holy Spirit gives us spiritual gifts for our kingdom tasks, including the gift of discernment.

> 1 Corinthians 12:10–11 "To another the working of miracles, to another prophecy, to another discerning of spirits, to another different kinds of tongues, to another the interpretation of tongues, [11]But one and the same Spirit

works all these things, distributing to each one individually as He wills."

Work in the full assurance that God's Word goes to the depths of the inner man to accomplish God's purpose.

> Hebrews 4:12 "For the Word of God is living and powerful and sharper than any two-edged sword, piecing even to the division of soul and spirit, and of joints and marrow, and is a discerner of the thoughts and intents of the heart."

And nothing is hidden from God.

> Hebrews 4:13 "And there is no creature hidden from His sight, but all things are naked and open to the eyes of Him to whom we must give account."

If a person is wavering because of doubt or a lapse of faith, we must ask God to help us be merciful and compassionate, just as God has been merciful and compassionate with us. We are called to do all we can to restore the individual who is in doubt. Then we can testify in the same manner as Paul.

> Philippians 1:12 "But I want you to know, brethren, that the things which happened to me have actually turned out for the furtherance of the gospel."

There is a distinction between those who desire to follow God but need instruction or encouragement and those who are rebellious. Paul explains this distinction to Timothy in regards to his own self.

> 1 Timothy 1:13 "Although I was formerly a blasphemer, a persecutor, and an insolent man; I did it ignorantly in unbelief."

Paul's conduct had been wrong, but it was not as if he had clearly understood the truth and profusely rebelled against Christ. God holds us responsible according to the degree of our knowledge of His will.

> Luke 12:47–48 (Jesus speaking) "And that servant who knew his master's will, and did not prepare himself or do according to his will, shall be beaten with many stripes. [48]But he who did not know, yet committed things deserving of stripes, shall be beaten with few. For everyone to whom much is given, from him much will be required; and to whom much has been committed, of him they will ask the more."

When God brings such a person into our sphere of influence, we are called to present the Gospel (Matthew 28:18–20, Mark 16:15–18) unless God clearly shows you not to. We can always present (open the word and let them read) God's Word and let the word of God carry out its purpose.

> Isaiah 55:11 "So shall My word be that goes forth from My mouth; It shall not return to Me void, But it shall accomplish what I please, And it shall prosper in the thing for which I sent it."

God's Word is far more powerful than anything we can say or do. We are to follow our calling, but people are free to choose, and not everyone will profit from the word of God.

> Hebrews 4:2 "For indeed the gospel was preached to us as well as to them; but the word which they heard did not profit them, not being mixed with faith in those who heard it."

So do not be discouraged.

Life Application Questions

- How can we, as vulnerable human beings, gain an understanding of God's expectations?
- How can we, as weak humans prone to sin, possibly expect to live up to God's expectations?
- Do you understand the distinctive difference between looking to God for answers and seeking God's strength and willingly choosing to do things your own way and/or rebel against God and His ways and plans for your life?
- What are you called to do in "making a distinction" as regards others?

Verse 23

"But others save with fear, pulling them out of the fire, hating even the garment defiled by the flesh."

But others save with fear

There is more than one category of people who are not walking in Truth. These others who Jude refers to could be those who are living in sin because of false teaching, dreamers, complainers and/or grumblers, mockers, the greedy, those who live in the lusts of the flesh, and maybe even the rebellious. This could include anyone around us. God wants that none should perish (2 Peter 3:9). We should seek to save them, fearing for their soul.

Pulling them out of the fire

This is a picture of a violent rescue. If you feared for someone's life because he was caught in a fire, you would act swiftly and forcefully to pull him out. This should be the Christian's attitude and action toward those who are in the process of being consumed by sin and false teaching and destined for the fires of hell.

The prophets of the Old Testament feared for the lives of the Israelites. They stepped into difficult and often violent situations to speak the words of truth that God called them to deliver.

> Luke 11:29–32 (Jesus speaking) "And while the crowds were thickly gathered together, He began to say, "This is an evil generation. It seeks a sign, and no sign will be given to it

except the sign of Jonah the prophet. [30]For as Jonah became a sign to the Ninevites, so also the Son of Man will be to this generation. [31]The queen of the South will rise up in the judgment with the men of this generation and condemn them, for she came from the ends of the earth to hear the Wisdom of Solomon; and indeed a greater than Solomon is here. [32]The men of Nineveh will rise up in the judgment with this generation and condemn it, for they repented at the preaching of Jonah; and indeed a greater than Jonah is here." (The full story of Jonah is found in the book of Jonah.)

Jesus faced opposition in many of the places God called Him to deliver a message to a lost and dying world.

John 8:26, 37 "I have many things to say and to judge concerning you, but He who sent Me is true and I speak to the world those things which I have heard from Him . . . . [37]I know that you are Abraham's descendants but you seek to kill me because My word has no place in you."

An example of this is when Jesus stepped into a volatile situation (the scribes and Pharisees were making accusations and had pulled the woman from her bed of sin) and faced the Scribes and Pharisees as He "pulled" the woman caught in sin from the "fire" of judgment.

John 8:7–11 "So when they continued asking Him (Jesus), He raised Himself up and said to them, "He who is without sin among you, let him throw a stone at her first." [8]And again He stooped down and wrote on the ground. [9]Then those who heard it, being convicted by their conscience, went out one by one, beginning with the oldest even to the last. And Jesus was left alone, and the woman standing in the midst. [10]When Jesus had raised Himself up and saw no one but the woman, He said to her, "Woman, where are those accusers of yours? Has no one condemned you?" [11]She said, "No one, Lord." And Jesus said to her, "Neither do I condemn you; go and sin no more.'"

And so did His disciples.

In Matthew, friends "pulled" the paralytic "from the fire" by acting swiftly and purposely to bring him to Jesus. This story is told in three of the Gospels: Matthew, Luke, and John, which means God placed an emphasis on this story and has something He wanted to impress upon the readers of His Word. He wants us to get the message.

> Matthew 9:2–8 "Then behold, they brought to Him a paralytic lying on a bed. When Jesus saw their faith, He said to the paralytic, 'Son, be of good cheer; your sins are forgiven you.' [3]And at once some of the scribes said within themselves, "This Man blasphemes!" [4]But Jesus, knowing their thoughts, said, "Why do you think evil in your hearts? [5]For which is easier, to say, 'Your sins are forgiven you,' or to say, 'Arise and walk'? [6]But that you may know that the Son of Man has power on earth to forgive sins"—then He said to the paralytic, "Arise, take up your bed, and go to your house." [7]And he arose and departed to his house. [8]Now when the multitudes saw it, they marveled[£] and glorified God, who had given such power to men." (See also Luke 5:17–26 and Mark 2:1–5 for this story.)

God blesses those who restore the wanderer.

> James 5:19–20 "Brethren, if anyone among you wanders from the truth, and someone turns him back, [20]let him know that he who turns a sinner from the error of his way will save a soul from death and cover a multitude of sins."

Hating even the garment defiled by the flesh

This refers to the effects and devastations of sin that defile. We should not hate a person who is deceived or caught up in sin. But we should certainly hate the effects and devastations of sin, that is, hate the sin and love the sinner.

Here again is a picture of one so close to the fire that the various destructive powers of that fire even ruins his very clothing.

It is possible that, in the process of seeking to rescue a brother or sister from sin, one becomes ensnared in sin himself.

> Galatians 6:1 "Brethren, if a man is overtaken in any trespass, you who are spiritual restore such a one in a spirit of gentleness, considering yourself lest you also be tempted."

Especially consider guarding your eye. Remember you are a lamp to be put upon a lampstand.

> Luke 11:33–36 (Jesus speaking) "No one, when he has lit a lamp, puts it in a secret place or under a basket, but on a lampstand, that those who come in may see the light. ³⁴The lamp of the body is the eye. Therefore, when your eye is good, your whole body also is full of light. But when your eye is bad, your body also is full of darkness. ³⁵Therefore take heed that the light which is in you is not darkness. ³⁶If then your whole body is full of light, having no part dark, the whole body will be full of light, as when the bright shining of a lamp gives you light."

Therefore, when attempting to rescue those caught up in sin, the Christian's attitude toward the enticement and effect of sin should be hate and consistency in seeking God's strength and wisdom. See the next verses.

Galatians 6:2–6 "Bear one another's burdens, and so fulfill the law of Christ. ³For if anyone thinks himself to be something, when he is nothing, he deceives himself. ⁴But let each one examine his own work, and then he will have rejoicing in himself alone, and not in another. ⁵For each one shall bear his own load. ⁶Let him who is taught the word share in all good things with him who teaches."

Above all else, pray.

James 5:16 "Confess your trespasses to one another, and pray for one another, that you may be healed. The effective, fervent prayer of a righteous man avails much."

Life Application Questions

- How do the words in this verse to "save with fear" apply to Christians living in the world today?
- Are there people around you who need you to take the initiative and pull them from the fire?
- What is the first step toward rescuing those who are perishing and caring for those who are headed for destruction?

Verse 24

"Now to Him who is able to keep you from stumbling, and to present you faultless before the presence of His glory with exceeding joy,"

Now to Him who is able to keep you from stumbling

This means falling into sin. Jude brings us encouraging words in the midst of these serious warnings. God is able to keep you! This is a powerful truth, which we must properly understand. This statement doesn't promise that, no matter what you do, you won't stumble. It does promise that God is able to keep you no matter where you are or what you are doing.

> Ephesians 3:20 "Now to Him who is able to do exceedingly abundantly above all that we ask or think according to the power that works in us."

Jude has already placed upon us the responsibility to "build ourselves up in the faith" (verse 20) and to "keep ourselves in the love of God" (verse 21). We have a clear responsibility to act according to the instructions of God's Word. But we are often instructed in God's Word to look to and depend upon God.

> Romans 13:14 "But put on the LORD Jesus Christ, and make no provision for the flesh, to fulfill its lusts."

> Proverbs 3:5–6 "Trust in the LORD with all your heart, and lean not on your own understanding; ⁶in all your ways acknowledge Him, and He shall direct your paths."

Micah 7:7 "Therefore I will look to the LORD; I will wait for the God of my salvation; My God will hear me."

John 6:40 "And this is the will of Him who sent Me, that everyone who sees the Son and believes in Him may have everlasting life; and I will raise him up at the last day."

Titus 2:13 "Looking for the blessed hope and glorious appearing of our great and Savior Jesus Christ."

Hebrews 12:2 "Looking unto Jesus, the author and finisher of our faith, who for the joy that was set before Him endured the cross, despising the shame, and has sat down at the right hand of the throne of God."

It is He who keeps us as we look to Him.

Isaiah 26:3–4 "You will keep him in perfect peace, whose mind is stayed on You, because he trusts in You. 4Trust in the LORD forever, for in YAH, the LORD, is everlasting strength."

Isaiah 45:22 "Look to Me, and be saved, all you ends of the earth! For I am God, and there is no other."

And to present you faultless

This means without sin, pure. This is the truth of Christianity, a blessing we can get no other way but by the grace of God. It is not within our own power to present ourselves faultless to God. God's grace, made available through the Gospel of Jesus Christ, assures we can be made righteous. If we accept the free gift offered to us under the grace and mercy of God, the righteousness of God is imputed to us.

2 Corinthians 5:21 "For He made Him who knew no sin to be sin for us, that we might be come the righteousness of God in Him."

This important concept separates true Christian doctrine from the doctrine of the cults and false teaching.

Titus 3:4–7 "But when the kindness and the love of God our Savior toward man appeared, ⁵not by works of righteousness which we have done, but according to His mercy He saved us, through the washing of regeneration and renewing of the Holy Spirit, ⁶whom He poured out on us abundantly through Jesus Christ our Savior, ⁷that having been justified by His grace we should become heirs according to the hope of eternal life."

Man is sinful, and God is holy. This is why, when it comes to approaching God, we must be presented faultless or not be presented at all.

Before the presence of his glory

The Scriptures teach that no one can stand in the presence of God's glory and live. God is Light and dwells in a unapproachable Light. In Him, there is no darkness. Until the completion of God's work in us we are not yet ready to live in eternity with Him. Another way to put this is that, in the presence of such an awesome and powerful God, our human frailty would become so evident that we could not even live. God knows this and would not even allow a saint like Moses to see His face. Moses saw only a fleeting glimpse of God's back.

Exodus 33:20 "But He said, "You cannot see My face; for no man shall see Me, and live."

John 1:18 "No one has seen God at any time. The only begotten Son, who is in the bosom of the Father, He has declared Him."

1 Timothy 6:16 "Who alone has immortality, dwelling in unapproachable light, whom no man has seen or can see, to whom be honor and everlasting power."

Immortality

He always existed and always will.

Unapproachable light

His majesty is too great for humans to see.

Everlasting

To God, we attribute the highest power that shall never cease.

With exceeding joy

What a wonderful thing that, not only will we be presented faultless before a holy God, we will be presented with exceeding joy by our Lord and Savior, Jesus Christ, who has bought us with His own lifeblood. It is both our joy and His. This is in great contrast to the fear and dread the wicked will experience when they stand before God on judgment day.

Life Application Questions

- What truth of Christianity is presented in this verse?
- What concept sets the truth of Christianity apart from false teachings and the doctrine of cults?
- Will you be able to be presented "faultless" before a Holy God?
- How can this be?

Verse 25

"To God our Savior, who alone is wise, be glory and majesty, dominion and power, both now and forever. Amen."

To God our Savior

God is the one and only Savior of our souls. We know there is only one true God. It is quite interesting, however, that the Scriptures also tell us that the LORD is the only Savior.

> Isaiah 43:11 "I, even I, am the LORD, and besides Me there is no savior."

> Hosea 13:4 "Yet I am the LORD your God ever since the land of Egypt, and you shall know no God but Me;"

The title of Savior is given to both God the Father and Jesus, but no one else.

> Titus 1:3 "God our Savior."

> Titus 1:4 "Christ our Savior."

> Titus 2:13 "Our great God and Savior Jesus Christ."

Who alone is wise

All true wisdom originates from God. Therefore, He alone is wise.

> Proverbs 2:6 "For the LORD gives wisdom; from His mouth come knowledge and understanding;"

> Proverbs 21:30 "There is no wisdom or understanding or counsel against the LORD."

> Romans 11:33 "Oh, the depth of the riches both of the wisdom and knowledge of God! How unreachable are His judgments and his ways past finding out!"

Be glory

This refers to praise, honor, dignity, and worship (be His or belong to Him).

> Romans 16:27 "To God, alone be glory through Jesus Christ forever."

> 1 Timothy 1:17 "Now to the King eternal, immortal, invisible, to God who alone is wise, be honor and glory forever and ever."

And majesty

This refers to magnificence or splendor (be His or belong to Him).

Dominion

This refers to power, control, and all authority over heaven and Earth and all that is or will ever be (be His or belong to Him).

And power

This refers to the ability and authority to choose and do (be His or belong to Him).

Both now and forever

This refers to past, present, and future. God will never lose these traits listed above. Unlike man, His nature and character does not change. As He is, so shall He always be!

Malachi 3:6 "For I am the LORD, I do not change;"

Amen

Thayer's Greek dictionary gives great insight to this little word at the beginning of a discourse—surely, truly, and of a truth at the end—so it is, so be it, and may it be fulfilled.

It was a custom passed over from the synagogues to the Christian assemblies that, when he who had read or discoursed had offered up solemn prayer to God, the others responded "Amen" and thus made the substance of what was uttered their own.

The word "amen" is a most remarkable word. It was transliterated directly from the Hebrew into the Greek of the New Testament and then into Latin and English and many other languages, so it is practically a universal word. It has been called the best-known word in human speech. The word is directly related (in fact, almost identical) to the Hebrew word for "believe" (*amam*) or faithful. Thus, it came to mean "sure" or "truly," an expression of absolute trust and confidence.

Life Application Questions

- Where does wisdom come from?
- What does it mean to you that God never has and never will change?
- Why do we say "amen" at the end of our prayers?
- What is the 11:45 Call?
- Is there anything you have read in *The 11:45 Call* or your additional studies regarding this topic that you will apply to your life?
- How will you go about making this change?

AFTERWORD

In the three years of writing this book, we have grown as teachers. We now understand why teachers are expected to write a book. It is a good way for God to stretch your capacity to let Him work and to enhance the two-way communication between you and Him. But it is a fine line between flesh and spirit, and they are so intertwined. Flesh must be submitted to God, and fleshly desires must be taken to the cross so a person may be used in the fullness of all God has planned for kingdom work.

We are presuming that God had us write about Jude because we needed the lessons that it contained. The areas of sinful action and thought are natural to our sin nature. Many of the things that are wrong in our lives, we have been taught by example from the cradle time of our lives. They are so much a part of our nature that separating them from our character is something that we can only accomplish with God's intervention and sustenance.

Even as we grew through the development of this work and as we wrote and taught from it, the development edit of the publishing process was where God really begin to say, "Dig in." Our prayer life increased substantially as the editing process moved forward.

The truth of Jude, a warning about false teachers, apostates and mockers, grumblers, and complainers, began to penetrate. We became so much more aware of the scriptural warning to teachers from James 3:1, that is, we will be held accountable and receive a stricter judgment. We didn't ask God for the gift of teaching. He freely gave it, and it has brought us to some level of maturity based on our willingness to submit to Him.

Teaching is a terribly irritating gift in the immature stages.

In 1996, when we stood in line to receive our M.Ed. diplomas, Dr. Jack Layman, our beloved professor, said "God grows things." We cannot forget that. This is not to say that we have grown at the rate God would have liked. But we have grown some in spite of our stubbornness and fleshly battles.

The areas that Jude warned about are becoming clearly engraved on our minds as we have probably read the material for this book hundreds of times, not to mention the number of times we have combed the research materials for answers. But we do not ever want to forget the hope that is within us.

At first, Jude's examples showed us areas where we felt pretty sure we were not in error, and then God would take us deeper and reveal our hearts. We want to reinstate these in abbreviation for our clarification and your edification on Jude's examples.

False teachers and/or leaders who sometimes used divine revelation as a guise to mislead the people were using these examples. They were also teaching and leading people in the same sinful activities as Scripture had already revealed to be wayward and that God had specifically demonstrated would lead to destruction.

Jude's Examples

1. Fallen angels, even angels who surrounded the throne of God, saw God face to face constantly, and were aware of the work of the Father, have served God constantly and ministered alongside of the Holy Spirit. Even they can fall and will suffer the consequences. So here we are humans with a sin nature. The only chance we have to please God is in His strength and power. But God is a God of second chances. Look at the Israelites in the example number three.

2. The folks of Sodom and Gomorrah were the example of the ultimate indulgence in flesh. We have not reached the level they did, but we still have the tendency to indulge the flesh on occasion. And in completing the work on this book, God showed us areas

of which we were not even aware, and He made us aware that one indulgence leads to another when the flesh has not been crucified with Christ on the cross. Self indulgence causes us to focus on self when we should be focused on God. We cannot serve two masters. If we focus (serve) on God, He will take care of the "self" for us.

3. The Israelites, complainers, and grumblers saw God's hand move in their lives. His presence was clearly with them as He delivered them from Pharaoh when they followed God's instructions. God parted the water, kept them in food and clothing that didn't wear out, and kept them safe in the wilderness. He even showed them His presence in a cloud by day and a fire by night. Yet they complained, couldn't trust God, and lost the blessing of living to enter the Promised Land. Think of it. They died in the wilderness when all of God's provisions were right there before them.

4. People are like Cain, who was self-serving and cared only for himself, greedy like Balaam, and rebellious like Korah.

5. Jude lists others: dreamers who live in their own dreamed-up world, brute beasts who do what comes naturally, mockers who walk according to their own ungodly lusts, and sensual persons who cause divisions. "But you" (me and we) are to submit to the will of the Father and His strength that keeps you on the path to righteousness. It is the duty of man to examine and prepare themselves (2 Corinthians 13) in order to live in the full blessings of spiritual health. 2 Corinthians 4 tells us that "even though this treasure is in earthen vessels (this is you) . . . it is the power of God at work" . . . "We are not to lose heart" . . . "even if our gospel is veiled" . . . "and the world has blinded our minds" . . . "Light shall shine out of darkness."

We must stop, look, and listen. We are called to "awaken from sleep (Romans 13:11, 1 Thessalonians 5:4–6)," "be alert (Matthew 24:42)" and "being sent out the midst of wolves . . . be wise as serpents and harmless as doves (Matthew 10:16)."

It is our duty to be aware, heed *The 11:45 Call*, and turn and walk in the new way (Hebrews 10:26). The call, to "contend earnestly for the faith (Jude 3)," is both personal and global. We are, after all, called to obey the commands of God, not man (Acts 5:29).

Our prayer for ourselves and you as readers is that we will allow God to continue to teach us so we will be strengthened to embrace our salvation, listen to the hope that is within us, seek first the kingdom of God and His righteousness, heed the warning, and flee from the devil.

We ask, LORD, please continue to bring people into our lives who will embrace us and hold us accountable to hold fast to the true faith, and we will not cause anyone to stumble. Help us to be found faithful and to diligently search for the Truth and accept nothing else. Help us to do the same for others so God's love may be manifested in our relationship. Amen.

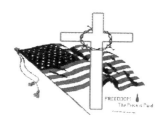

About the Authors

Who Are These Sheep? Where Have They Been?

Joel and Brenda Blakely, co-authors of *The 11:45 Call*, are blessed with five children, four in-laws, and six wonderful grandchildren who have made their lives both a joy and a challenge-to live out their faith before them.

They heard the Shepherd's voice, "Come, follow me," in the early 1990s. Following Him brought a radical lifestyle change, and it was the beginning of an incredible journey. As they filled the usual roles in their local church, preparation had just begun. The Shepherd began teaching them to "feed His sheep."

First, He took them to the Rock House, an inner-city street ministry crowded with children, although the ministry was supposed to be only for adults. The pastor looked at Brenda and Joel and said, "You are called here to start the Children's Ministry." With God's grace, Charlie, the bus driver and all-around minister, and great volunteers, it happened!

God had prepared the experience. It started in a non-air-conditioned ten-by-twelve room on a hot August evening with twenty-five hot, hungry, inner-city children. All were totally dependent on God's guidance and anointing for each moment.

He gave them an experience of seeing God do the "loaves and fishes." One small plate of sandwiches and a bottle of Coke were brought to feed the fifty-plus children at a party scheduled that day. Everyone had plenty, and even a sandwich was left over. It was a full and blessed three years of frontline experience with God.

God used everything they had learned and all they had experienced in their years of service as AIM youth camp counselors and church workers. They had been issued "calls" at AIM camps that changed their life course.

God blessed them as they completed undergraduate studies and began their graduate studies, but He had another plan. He led them to leave hearth, home, and family to go to school in another state. God's footsteps were very clear at Columbia International University in Columbia, South Carolina. These two very different people were tuned to work as one, as God had planned. God gave them the "Freedom, the Price is Paid" logo and began to make this truth real in their lives. The Bible curriculum course taken by Brenda under Mary Faith Phillips made a huge impact on both their lives.

The school administration helped them to develop their curriculum to complete their master's degrees in Christian school administration and let God design their internship. Once they had a good picture of the administration and operation of ministries and Christian schools, they followed Him on the road, visiting and learning from twenty-eight different organizations who were generous in their sharing and passing on the lessons learned from their experiences.

They were given the tasks of seeing how ministry work is done: what works, what does not work, and how to live by the government regulations in the seven different states in which they worked. The workshop, "Green Pastures and Red Tape," was just one of the many blessings God poured out from these opportunities.

After graduation in 1996, the journey continued as they were called to help Country Legend Camp, the Dunlap Youth Home, and Fireside Academy in their start-up. Then they spent time at the King's Ranch learning, sharing, and praying. After leaving the ranch, God put on their hearts to continue to pray for the administration of the ranch for the next ten years. Those prayers were answered as Elijah House prayer ministry replaced the Boys Town Program they had been using at the ranch.

A faithful friend and coworker at the ranch had brought Elijah House Prayer Ministry into their lives. God used Elijah House biblical principles to bring great changes into Joel and Brenda's lives. The LORD finally said, "Follow Me to Mississippi."

Junction Ridge Camp Management, Inc., was formed during the miraculous fourteen months they spent sitting on 186 acres of campground serving Mountain Movers Ministries. God had so beautifully created this place for them to earn their next degree.

At "Desert U" (Numbers 33:1–50), God got down in the trenches with them to uniquely equip and prepare them for what He had ahead. He reduced the curriculum down to fourteen months. He had things for them to do.

Rising to the challenge of working with a severe lack of funds gave them the opportunity to develop a closer walk with the Shepherd. The curriculum required them to have no other priority but to listen and learn.

Next, He led them to Sylvan Learning Center, where they served as teachers and then directors. When they applied for the position at the center, the owner told them, "This is meant to be." They helped rework the organizational structure and hired and trained new staff to make the center more effective in its mission. After this, the Shepherd led them on the next step in their walk of faith.

To fulfill a vision seen at the Kings Ranch to allow mothers to live in residence and raise their own children with help and guidance, God led them to the Baptist Children's Village (BCV) to help start the Residential Family Ministry. While at BCV, they also traveled on days off to work with Project Light in Lineville, Alabama. They helped them prepare documentation to expand Project Light into an international ministry and create the Community Multimedia Factory alongside Jim Crawford, Project Light's founder.

Next, they began working for clients in rural areas, who needed help to write grants, develop programs, and coordinate and administrate projects. Often the first words from the client were, "You are an answer to our prayers." This really put the Blakelys on the spot.

When you are an answer to prayer, they learned it is best to follow God through the process. This work led them to the Mississippi

Natural Products Initiative. Projects initiated here brought hope and help to small farmers.

Thanks to the Blakely's Sunday School class, the Raymond Road Learning Center became a reality in 2006. This provided an opportunity to use the Project Light Curriculum and other programs the Blakely's respected for their proven success. For the next two years, they were blessed by serving the learners and the volunteers who brought hope to the learners.

In January 2008, they set up a northern office in the Spring Hill Schoolhouse in Eupora, Mississippi. Brenda began work for a Eupora architectural firm as a grant writer, and within three weeks of their arrival, they knew they were called to go to Westwood Baptist Mission. This growing time brought them into writing projects together and expanded their ministry opportunities.

The teaching opportunity at the mission, often referred to as "Miracleland," spurred the development of Expository Bible Studies and numerous topical Bible lessons. They also were able to use their Elijah House facilitator training in classes here and in the area.

They learned that following Him means being "wise as a serpent and harmless as a dove." It means trusting and obeying, and it means an incredible adventure.

Now that Jude is in the publisher's hands, the Blakelys are seeking God's leading in editing and recording the Expository Bible Study, *James Sets the Plumb Line*. *Peter's Pastoral Principles* is in the development stage. Joel teaches it at the mission's Sunday Bible study class, and the class contributes.

Joel and Brenda say, "Thank you, LORD, for the opportunity to serve." They know it is only by His strength they have been able to follow Him and by His grace and mercy they are learning to feed His sheep. They pray, asking, "LORD may all who come behind us find us faithful" (Hebrews 12:1).

Made in the USA
Lexington, KY
15 April 2015